LETTERS FROM PAUL CLAUDEL, MY GODFATHER

LETTERS FROM PAUL CLAUDEL, MY GODFATHER

By Sister Agnes du Sarment

Translated by William Howard, Earl of Wicklow

THE NEWMAN PRESS ℕ𝔻 WESTMINSTER, MARYLAND · 1964

First printing 1964

This translation was made from *Lettres inedites de mon Parrain, Paul Claudel,* published by J. Gabalda, Paris France, 1963.

Nihil obstat: JOHANNES CHISHOLM, C.S.Sp.
              Censor Deputatus

Imprimatur: JOANNES CAROLUS
            Archiepiscopus Dublinen
            Hiberniae primas
            Die 14 November 1962

[ ]

CONTENTS

[ ]

A BIOGRAPHICAL SKETCH

WHEN PAUL CLAUDEL died in February 1955, in his eighty-seventh year, an obituary described him as the last surviving member of the remarkable triad which had dominated French literature during the period between the two great wars. The other two members, Valery and Gide, had each lived on to considerable ages, but were men, especially the latter, of very different types, who may have thought their outlooks were far more original than his, but who did, in fact, conform far more closely to the mental habits of the age. Just as Claudel was less influenced by the prevailing fashions of thought, if indeed he was influenced at all, so it is likely that his work will endure more solidly. He has been described as "the poet of joy, robust, exuberant"—qualities which are not always to be found even in the Christian literature of our day.

He was born at Villeneuve-sur-Fère on August 6th, 1868, and grew up in a family which was not perhaps unbelieving, but certainly not very practicing in religious matters; he refers to this in one of the letters in this book, for he had considerable difficulty with them on this account, as did his correspondent whom he wished to encourage. As a boy and as a young man he remained more or less indifferent to religion, but while still very young he was converted to Christianity in a very definite way; Paul Claudel was never an indefinite character. After the first and unexpected flash of light it took him four years to come to a final decision, but when this was finally made, it was all the more certain because of the hesitation and the delay which had gone before. Great minds do not usually move by leaps and bounds, though there may be moments on the way when the mists lift and for a time they have a glimpse of their goal; it will be remembered that the final stage in Newman's journey lasted roughly four years.

There was something that could almost be called concrete about the first intimation that Claudel received. It was on a Christmas Day, during Vespers in the Cathedral of Notre-Dame de Paris, when he was standing "near the second pillar from the entrance to the chancel, on the right side where the sanctuary is," that he suddenly began to believe. We are told that he had been prepared for this belief by reading Rimbaud, the writer who had more influence on his thought than any other, and also by the death of his grandfather from cancer—as regards this latter, French Catholics are perhaps a little too ready to establish close connections between religion and ill-health; it remains true that to have a *mens sana in corpore sano* is still permissible for a Christian.

During the four formative years which followed, he derived much help from reading Aristotle and Dante, Pascal and Bossuet, and perhaps rather strangely, the humble hidden stigmatist, Anne-Catherine Emmerick. He was also starting to give out as well as to receive, for he was at work on the early versions of his first plays, *Tete d'Or* and *La Ville*, which have been described as strange and obscure works, belonging to the Symbolist tradition. The first hints rather vaguely at the Christian solution for an individual destiny, while the second widens this destiny* to being that of the whole of society.

Claudel is best known in the English-speaking world for two other plays. First there is *L'Annonce faite a Marie*, The Tidings Brought to Mary, which has been translated into most European languages, and has been produced several times in English, when it had no small success and caused much discussion and interest. It first appeared in New York in 1923. The second is *Le Soulier de Satin*, The Satin Slipper, which has not to the present writer's knowledge been produced in English, but thirty years ago was translated by the late Monsignor John O'Connor, the Father Brown of G. K. Chesterton's detective stories, and was acclaimed by most of the English-speaking critics at the time. The letters in this book give an interesting and unpublished account of the production of these two plays in French.

* See the very remarkable appreciation of Claudel and his work, written just after his death, by Earnest Beaumont, which appeared in the *Tablet*, March 5, 1955, Vol. 205, No. 5989.

There are two other plays which did much to establish Claudel's reputation as a dramatic poet, *L'Otage* and *Partage du Midi*. In spite of the fact that in *Partage du Midi* the poet reaches some of the profoundest depths of human feeling, these two plays have not got the broad scope of *Le Soulier de Satin*, a long dramatic poem which can claim a high place in modern literature. This drama, with its sixteenth century setting of Spain as the Catholic power in the new world, "is that of all mankind," as Earnest Beaumont wrote,* "or at least of that part of mankind at all conscious of its own nature and its own destiny."

If, however, Paul Claudel is best known in the English-speaking world for two of his plays, in France his fame rests above all on his lyrical poems. The most important of these are without doubt the *Cinq Grandes Odes*. If he may perhaps be accused of a tendency not unknown among his fellow-countrymen, that towards grandiloquence, then we must grant that it belongs to the grand manner, and that as did Victor Hugo he is able to combine it with passages of the finest and most authentic poetry. To quote Beaumont once more: "He is a poet of great originality. His verse, which as he says has neither 'rhyme nor metre,' is extremely flexible and he ranges from a vivid colloquialism to a biblical sublimity, with majestically sweeping rhythms and sustained metaphors."

Paul Claudel was however something much more than a highly gifted playwright and poet and man

* See the *Tablet*, March 5, 1955.

of letters, a talent and calling which can lead to a certain narrowness and preoccupation with self, at the risk of yielding, usually at the expense of all humor, to the error of producing art for art's sake. Not so Claudel. He was a French patriot in the best sense of that much abused word, who served his country as an increasingly eminent public figure throughout a long life, at the end of which he was described in an obituary as "a vital force in France." It was not merely his writings which were vital.

As a young man he studied law and political science, but in 1890, the year of his return to the Church, he entered the diplomatic service, and started by working in consulates in New York, Boston and China. At the time of his second appointment to China he married Renée-Marie Perrin; several of the letters which follow bear witness to the happiness and serenity of his family life as he moved on into old age. He was destined to rise high in his profession, perhaps at no small sacrifice to himself, for his letters seem to tell of a sense of exile as he served his country in such distant places, of nostalgia for his native land. There is perhaps no human, certainly no European race, who are so attached to their *patrie* as the French, sometimes with a puzzling insularity pervading their continental status. Their empire-builders have traveled far, but they are not by nature a traveling people. Claudel was Ambassador to Japan from 1921 to 1925, and recorded many of his experiences in *The East I Know*; from 1927 to 1933 he was Ambassador to the United States, and some of his personal, at times unexpected reactions to that great country, are described in the letters that follow. As he grew older he was moved to less exacting work in Belgium, where he remained as Ambassador until he retired in 1936.

Though a highly successful diplomat, he had a reputation for brusqueness and lack of tact. This showed itself in his relations with Gide, who at one time gave signs of being attracted away from his unfortunate life towards the Christian camp. Gide seems to have taken fright at the rock-like quality of Claudel's convictions; maybe Claudel acted quite rightly, and it will be remembered that his patron, St. Paul, could scarcely be described as a tactful man. Very different were his relations with Jacques Rivière, but we can leave it to the authoress of this book to give us fresh light on that well-known story. As regards his brusqueness, these letters have something very different to tell, with their account of his kindness and courtesy for a young Parisian student whose importunity, though flattering, may well have been quite an embarrassment. One is reminded of Dr. John in his gentle moments, and they were not so rare as all that.

WILLIAM HOWARD
Earl of Wicklow

[ ]

PREFACE

PAUL CLAUDEL had not given up his ideas of the monastic life, to which he believed in his youth that he had been called, without a certain bitterness. On several occasions he described how the answer he received from God at Ligugé was No, and he told Sister du Sarment of this.

When Jean Amrouche wished to understand how he had come to hear this "no," Claudel admitted that the reply did not exactly come to him in words, but held that it was not the less definite at the level of the interior life.

Well, as far as I could see, Claudel was not altogether resigned that God should not accept him to be among the monks of St. Benedict, those men who have placed all their trust in the Patriarch.

> "Rather than struggle against the world,
> it is more simple not to look at it
> And to put on the cowl."

He had no regrets, I agree, but he was not happy at this transient exclusion. He retained his load of genius, of which he had thought he could rid himself, to benefit along with the other members from the graces of community life. He remained in the world, without however becoming much attached to it. For though more than any other poet he may have appreciated the valuable things it had to offer, so full of promise, it was with the sole object of bringing them into the service of the One Being who had created them. He only found them of such interest because they bore, negatively yet for all to see, the divine seal and signature.

Claudel was not to have a place in choir, but wherever he went at the orders of his government—to the Far East, to America, to Denmark or Central Europe, finally in Belgium—this diplomat was always to be found, as in France, part of the Holy Sacrifice offered in praise to the same God.

*   *   *

When he met this young girl, he was glad to see her setting out in the right direction—along the way of God, the "true way" above all others, leading to that end which is also the beginning. *Ego sum Principium et Finis.* When he visited the Béguinage later, to be present at her profession, he was conscious of a deeper emotion. She was indeed not a Béguine, this little Sister who was to call herself his god-child, but belonged to the community which has replaced those remarkable women who played such a leading part in Flemish and Rhenish mysticism. In their Béguinage, that fascinating quadrangle of silence which gives the authentic effect of a Memling, these *Filles de l'Eglise,* with Sister du Sarment among them, have their convent of prayer and sanctification.

I came to know Sister du Sarment in Paris, under another name. Claudel had just opened for her the gate of light. Like all awakened souls she was seeking for her vocation. She needed solitude and she loved the mystery of poetry which gives to art its living form. We suggested she should visit Bruges and she resolved to settle there. It was a haven of grace for that generous soul. The story which is told us by the author of this book amply proves it. We can understand how, when she entered the religious life, in which everything tends to be more intense than in a life less based on one center, this friendship which grew up between her and her great poet Paul Claudel became especially highly developed and took on a most detailed form. The soul of Claudel felt serene as he thought of his brothers and sisters praying for him during those hours when the conditions of his life kept him from his Lord. Little Sister du Sarment, who understood her art so well and was able to bring him with such advantage into the traditional liturgy, was able to cheer his solitude.

The fact was that this famous man, surrounded by children and grandchildren, who was at an advanced age receiving all the honors, had become as solitary in spirit not as some Benedictine monk, a cenobite, but as a complete *monk,* let us say a hermit. If there was a Béguine in the world inhabited by this ambassador and most real of poets, it was this soul, which had little contact with his nearest and dearest and even less with his neighbors—a *Fils de l'Eglise* however— the soul of Paul Claudel.

STANISLAS FUMET

"Lord you have placed in me a seed not of death but of light"

⟦ ⟧

INTRODUCTION

THIS STORY began thirty-eight years ago. I have told it many times and it has always met with deep and warm feelings. Many who have heard it have joyfully urged me on. "You absolutely must publish this."

While I agreed with them, I found the idea painful, making public these deep and intimate facts which have made up the pattern of my life. But the day came when, yielding to a final request, I decided to take up my pen. May I please be excused for writing all through in the first person? If I tried to present this story in an impersonal way, this would take away all its life, all its authenticity.

For thirty years I had the happiness to enjoy the friendship of Paul Claudel, and the immense help and kindness I received from him have made me hope that by publishing these pages I may attract and perhaps increase the attachment of my readers to him, so that they also may receive that seed "not of death but of light" which has been able to transform and to illumine a whole life. Need I say that the secret of this "light" was not to be found in us, but in that other one of whom we always spoke, Christ, who helped me to find this unique friendship and who was its life throughout the long years.

Neither has death brought anything to an end between us. It merely removed the obstacle of bodily distance.

SO KIND AND CRUEL

IT WAS ON January 5, 1926, that I met him for the first time. By what providential chance . . . a young girl from the provinces, studying in Paris, unknown, with no claim on him and without any introduction, or any literary contacts—face to face with a man who was well known throughout the whole world. I can only see in this the will of God, who was the guide in this happy encounter up to the end.

At this time Claudel was at last beginning to emerge from the semi-obscurity in which he had been left for thirty years by an uncomprehending and materialistic generation.

Le Soulier de Satin[1] was just being published (it first appeared with *Le Roseau d'Or*) and Claudel was fifty-seven years old; he was at the height of his maturity but the world was not yet mature enough to accept him. He was to wait for almost twenty years before public opinion at last acknowledged his genius.

On my side, I knew nothing of him as a man, ex-

[1] *The Satin Slipper*, a play translated into English by John O'Connor, and published by Sheed & Ward.

cept that he was the Ambassador of France in Japan, and of his works at the most two or three, which I had only half-understood but which had made a great impression on me.

It was not long before I had started reading the poet's work. This had been going on for some months, after I had met a friend who was trying his hand at literature and who in the midst of the tumultuous quarter around the Opera House had been telling me of Maritain and Massis. He had spoken of the recent death of Jacques Rivière, on February 14, 1925. The death of Rivière was, in the long run, the starting point of this great adventure which is still going on.

At the time, that seductive Gide was attracting the young, so easily fascinated by that cunning pen which was able to sow such baleful seeds. For a time I was myself seduced by the glamour of those gorgeous, faultless sentences—with their concealed poison.

In the troubles of the adolescence through which I was passing, I thought it was there that I would find the light I was searching for with such difficulty. Besides, as is the way with all young people, the most advanced theories were those which had the most success. That winter of 1924 to 1925 was full of darkness and uncertainty; the smallest thing was enough to lead me astray.

Then God intervened in clear and splendid fashion, and by such simple means that as I look back over the years I am amazed at what he did.

After my First Communion I had gradually lost my faith. None of those around me, whether they belonged to my family or my school life, were practicing Christians. Now and then a few fragments of prayers would find their way back to my lips, but the atmosphere of the Schools and of the Sorbonne managed to drive into almost complete oblivion what stock of religious knowledge I had as a child.

Now, on the night of that chance meeting near the Opera House, I was astonished to feel an inward urge to pray. I stammered out an Our Father and a Hail Mary, the only prayers which had survived.

Every night, impelled by the same dark impulse within me, I repeated those two prayers almost unwittingly. A few weeks later, in the same state of mind I was surprised to find myself saying the words "I believe"—though at the time they seemed to have no meaning. Only several years later did I understand the secret and ineffable touch that conquered me, or rather, won me back. This time the victory was final.

It is easy to imagine the strange situation in which I found myself. What then was this unknown Presence which had appeared within me? How was I to respond? I was trying to find my way, without advice or support, in a foreign world, without any idea where I could go for light.

God would provide.

A man had started home from the most distant parts of the Far East, returning to his country after a long absence: Paul Claudel, Ambassador of France, coming back from Tokyo. Calling at a port he heard that his young friend, Jacques Rivière, was dead, and his first object was to visit Isabelle and give her the collection of letters her husband had written to him from 1907 to 1914.

"Do what you like with them," he said to her.

Jacques, on his side, had kept Claudel's letters carefully, so his widow was able to put together a long and fascinating exchange of views. It first appeared, in fragments, in the *Nouvelle Revue Française*.

If we turn to this valuable correspondence we find that Rivière disclosed to his friend, in three successive letters, the disturbed eagerness of his twenty years, and made known to him the religious struggle through which he was passing.

I was also little more than twenty years old, and these troubles were strangely like my own. Thus, I found my way into this correspondence by a very personal channel . . . I wanted to know how Claudel would reply to us.

Would he, a successful man already a master of his art and Consul at Tien-Tsin, look down condescendingly on the sometimes foolish anxiety of this young man? Would he be prepared to answer . . . and if he did so, would it be with authority and self-importance? The Consul of France almost claimed to be an experienced theologian. One of his letters was harshly dogmatic in tone . . .

But suddenly, the true Claudel, the man, came to life. He read this adolescent letter near the cradle of his little Marie, born but a short time before. He felt the beating of this "little heart like a rose." He held in his arms this little bundle "fresher than a bunch of white lilies,"[1] and now, as he himself described, a change had come in his relations with other human beings, for he was the father of one of them.[2]

He replied to Rivière with a feeling that was quite new to him for, dazzled with his own fatherhood, he used the words "My dear child." These first words of his came straight from the heart, words which the priest says to a penitent, which the good Lord will say when we reach the other world, which so many fathers are unable to say for the first time on earth without a tremor running through their whole being.

We can imagine their effect on a disturbed young man who had lost his way in the world. He must have had a sense of peace and security, of kindness and affection.[3]

Even if he had answered with no more than these three words, Rivière's soul, in spite of all the complications which he would yet be able to devise, had grasped the strong hand which the older man was

[1] Cinq Grandes Odes, Magnificat, p. 103.
[2] idem.
[3] In the Rivière-Fournier correspondence, Vol. III, p. 146, Rivière alludes to this letter: "He is so infinitely kind and cruel at the same time."

with such simplicity holding out to him from one continent to another.[1]

I lay so much stress on the drama of Jacques Rivière, because my own hand was to be placed where his was when he started, and because it was through him that I had my first personal contact with Paul Claudel.

Our first contact was like that between him and Rivière: this remote but reliable man offered his hand to the inexperienced child that I was, without realizing he was doing so, a kind paternal hand which he would not withdraw and would still hold out affectionately even when death had taken him away.

From that time onwards the way to God became clearer. A man of faith was answering all the questions which were troubling me, the more effectively because he was speaking to someone else. My free will, of which every adolescent is so jealous, was not being coerced—I could take what I wanted from his opinions and his advice. The complete liberty of judgment and action which this allowed me gave my conversion a stability which nothing could shake. It was before God alone, with him before my conscience, and with the advice and enlightenment given by one whom I had freely accepted, that I allowed myself to be won over progressively by grace. If I had been influenced by some merely human enthusiasm, my resolve would have wavered during the

---

[1] The Claudel-Rivière correspondence has been published in English by Burns & Oates under the title *Letters to a Doubter*.

difficult times to come. I was able to make my way
to God in straightforward fashion, firm in my convictions.

As this absorbing correspondence only appeared
in fragments in the *Nouvelle Revue Française*, I was
eagerly on the look-out for the Claudel-Rivière dialogue. Without being aware of it, I was slipping
from the Rivière into the Claudel camp—so much
so that within six months, while visiting a friend in
the Touraine, I found the courage to take a decisive
step in the direction of the Church, and asked if I
could speak to a priest.

August 24, the feast of Saint Bartholomew, was
decided on for my confession. I can never forget how
deeply moved I was that morning as I furtively slipped
out of the house and made my way to the little
country church where the priest was waiting for me,
or the unexpected joy with which I heard him invite
me to receive Holy Communion.

God has many ways of drawing souls to himself.
He often attracts them by means of the Eucharist
and sometimes arouses in them an almost unquench-
able thirst. How great a reward is given, however, to
souls which allow themselves to be conquered and
suddenly find that they have been submerged by an
immense Presence. The whole of heaven seems to be
holding a feast day and to be singing in unison with
their joy.

During the months that followed I gradually returned to the practice of a Christian life, while I kept

my mind sustained with the reading of the *Cinq Grands Odes*. The style, the vocabulary and the rhythm of the poem were all quite new to me. Nobody among those around me could give me the key; I found the author's thought difficult to understand, yet I was aware of being uplifted by those great lyrical waves. They had such a triumphant note running through them, the air breathed was so fresh, that I had an almost physical sense of deliverance when reading *l'Esprit et l'Eau*.

It was not just my Hellenic aspirations which found an echo in these impressive and dazzling odes, for they had a sparkling, spiritual quality which could not be resisted. Did not that *Magnificat* belong to me? And that *heavy golden censer packed with incense and embers*[1]—wasn't that my own heart carried along in an invisible hand in a nameless vortex of praise? *May you be blessed, oh my God! for you have delivered me from the idols . . . I am caught and cannot escape, like a figure captive in a sum.*

This "sum" was the Church, which had welcomed me like the mother of a prodigal child. I was glad to be her captive . . . *that prison which is the Light.*[2] I had become, almost, the Christian *who feels the throb of All Saints' Day from all her living brothers.*[3]

---

[1] . . . *pesant encensoir d'or tout bourre d'encens et de braise.* Cinq Grandes Odes, p. 84.

[2] *Cette prison qui est la Lumiere.* Corona benignitatis anni Dei, p. 162.

[3] . . . *qui sent palpiter la Toussaint de tous ses frères vivants.* Odes, p. 88.

As for the encounter with the Muse who is Grace, certainly this had happened to me. It was this Muse who had said to me, *It is not you who chose me, it is I who chose you before you were born.*[4] Now, at peace after a hard fight, I could answer:

Oh security and vastness of my domain! Oh dear universe between my hands that know![5] All my deepest feelings, even the most turbulent, found splendor in those serene poems with their vast expanse.

*   *   *

[4] *Ibid.*, p. 142.
[5] *O certitude et immensité de mon domaine! O cher univers entre mes mains connaissantes! Ibid.* p. 159.

2

THE FIRST THING

ONE UNDRAMATIC December day, something dramatic happened. I was reading a newspaper in the Metro and this headline caught my eye: "Claudel in Paris." It gave me a start and I found it hard to believe. Could it be that this man, whose thought had held me for months, and whom I had never expected to see, was no longer on the shores of the Pacific but here, near the banks of the quiet Seine which I was crossing? In a moment I had decided to do all I could in order to see him, to tell him how grateful I was. But how? There was nobody who could advise me, let alone introduce me or speak to him on my behalf. The first thing was to find out his address. I went into a bookshop near the Rue de Rennes, bought some little book and then, in a tone that I tried hard to make calm and indifferent, put the question.

"Madame, could you give me Paul Claudel's address?"

"Paul Claudel's address? But, my *dear* . . . we never give the addresses of authors. You must write to his publishers and they will forward the letter."

Then, as she saw my abashed look, though she continued to grumble she took up an office diary and opened it at random. On the page I was able to read, "Paul Claudel, 80 Rue de Passy." Providence was surely acting more and more kindly. I returned home, but now what? Should I go and ask to see him? I would never have dared without a letter of introduction. I decided to send him a note, for the pen has courage where the lips fail, but in order to find out where he was I made my way to the Rue de Passy.

The ordinary, unpretentious appearance of the house reassured me. But I was still too hesitant to make inquiries. Suddenly, I found myself, I don't really know how, face to face with the caretaker.

"Can I do anything for you, Mademoiselle?"

No going back now. "Monsieur Claudel . . . yes, he lives here, first floor on the right, but he will be leaving again in a few days."

This time, there was no time to lose. I went as fast as I could to the post office in the Place Chopin, and there, amid all the hubbub of the crowd, standing at a desk, with a curious mixture of enthusiasm and alarm, I wrote the most important letter of my life.

Paris
December 30, 1925

Dear Sir,

It is with some emotion that I venture to write to you. I have come to this sudden decision because of the news that you will soon be leaving Paris, and because I am more than ever aware of the debt I owe to you.

It is a humble debt, but one which I feel bound to pay, a debt of gratitude to the great Christian that you are.

Without being aware of it you have made me a convinced Christian. Your *Correspondance* with Jacques Rivière, published this summer in the *Nouvelle Revue Française*, came at a moment when, though my unbelief had been seriously shaken, I yet lacked the guidance to be completely converted, and was held back by unusual human respect from asking the Church for help and advice.

Did your arguments, when faced with Rivière's intellectual doubts, really have the most effect on me? I think your influence really has a wider compass and a deeper source. This makes it more real and more decisive: the one fact that you are deeply Christian, that Christianity is the very substance of your life, that *it is not the assent of our taste which you desire to win over, but our souls, so as to give them to God.*

If this is your dearest wish, and I am certain of this, then you will surely be willing to receive the homage of a soul whom you have helped God rescue.

This debt, which I am so glad to pay, is not merely the expression of my pen or my lips. This morning, having been granted the grace to receive Holy Communion, I said a prayer, as I always do, for you and for our departed Rivière.

May I now venture to ask you to show that you are not annoyed by this letter—by giving me the joy to express my gratitude in person, even if only by shaking your hand with affection, as the hand of a father to whom I owe much?

Might I call tomorrow, Thursday, about half-past two,

and have the honor and pleasure of being received by you?

I am hoping so much you will allow this, and meanwhile please be assured of my gratitude.

In order to gain time I sent this letter by express.[1] Shyness certainly had a restraining effect on my enthusiasm, but it is worth noting that though I had not yet met him, I gave the title of "father" to this man, and since then I have always spoken to him in this way. It can be seen that it was not the arguments of a man of letters which had influenced me, but the faith of a convinced Christian.

The next day, a Japanese in a blue livery with brass buttons opened the door, but as I should have expected, his master, who had not yet heard from me, was not at home. I was to wait, then, for his summons. In order to avoid difficulties with my family, I had given Claudel a friend's address. Two days later she came to see us and furtively slipped a blue envelope into my hand. I shall never forget the agitation with which I read his reply, after my friend had left, but it was to give me real joy. Let it speak for itself.

80 Rue de Passy
January 1, 1926

Mademoiselle,

Letters like yours, as you can well imagine, are a great

---

[1] As Claudel kept a large part of my letters, I have been able to collect together most of the correspondence, thanks to the kindness of his son Pierre.

joy for a Christian. A soul which has been saved and which will be a source of life, light and salvation to others is something beyond all price. What a New Year present you are giving me.

I was out yesterday but please come when you like, either about ten o'clock in the morning, or if you prefer, tomorrow or the next day at a quarter-past two. I look forward both to meeting you and congratulating you.

Believe me, I am

Yours most sincerely,

P. CLAUDEL

I felt quite bewildered. He said "as you can well imagine." But indeed I had never imagined this "great joy" and even less that I would be congratulated. The rôles were actually being reversed, and it is easy to understand how hard it was to restrain my enthusiasm.

On the morning of January 5 I rang the bell once again in the Rue de Passy. The same man opened the door and led me through one or two anterooms, furnished with Chinese lacquer, till we reached a large living room, its walls hung with mirrors. My heart was beating furiously. After a few moments, the blue livery reappeared and led me into yet another room from which I could hear a deep-pitched voice speaking . . . His? It was.

The door opened at last, and there he was, broad shouldered, straightforward blue eyes, forehead like a Roman arch . . . and that powerful jaw. Obviously, I never said a quarter of what I intended, but I told him of all the things which had led me to him. He asked me how I spent my time, and all about my family. He then spoke to me of Isabelle Rivière, thinking that I knew her. By a happy coincidence she was a near neighbor of the friend who had allowed me to use her address. Claudel asked me to take charge of a message for Isabelle, adding that I could either leave it with the concierge or take it myself, as I thought fit. I need not say how delighted I was to have this chance of meeting Jacques Rivière's widow. This was the first joy (and there were to be so many others) I received as a result of my meeting with the poet. Isabelle became my best friend and gave me much wise advice during those early years after my conversion. I have more to tell about her later.

Just as I was about to say goodbye, Claudel said to me, guessing a thought which I had not dared to put into words, "You would perhaps like to have a photograph?" He opened the drawer of a little table and there burst out a collection of photographs of every size and kind. Delighted, I chose . . . the largest (so large, in fact, that when I got home I had difficulty finding a place for it). Claudel wrote a dedication on it and I left, happy and satisfied but with no idea that this meeting would lead to anything further. I had expressed my gratitude, had been given the interview for which I was hoping, and expected nothing more.

3

A FRIEND OF CLAUDEL'S

I BEGAN THINKING things over with the restraint of one whose desires were still strictly limited, and who was unaware that God has boundless ambitions in his love for us and in the blessings he showers on us. On this occassion he was to show me what wide views he took as to the consequences of this meeting. Furthermore, no one can enter the orbit of a major star without being diverted from his course. It would have been necessary, as Jacques Rivière exclaimed in an almost despairing tone to Alain Fournier, "to see on a greater scale than Claudel," in order to escape from his ascendancy.

A fine track of light had opened before me, but I was to follow it with my eyes closed. Guided, maybe, by "a little invisible stone" . . . the lost bead of a rosary. Claudel had repaired its chain. Who had placed it in my hand? Perhaps my Guardian Angel, imitating that of *Prouhèze*. Now I possessed *that treasured tear, that diamond without flaw, that unique pearl, in the absence of which the whole rosary of the heavens would be destroyed.*[1]

[1] The Satin Slipper.

On the other side of the world, beyond the oceans, the poet was carrying the golden thread of my destiny to the islands of the East. A few months later, he received a letter in Tokyo.

This was his reply. . . .

FRENCH EMBASSY TO JAPAN
Tokyo
June 24, 1926

My Dear,

I have not forgotten you and it moves me to think you sometimes say a prayer for me. I am also happy to know that you persevere along the hard and lonely road of the Cross of Christ. Difficult as it often is for a man, it must be even more so for a woman; it certainly would be so if we did not have the consolation now and then of the good we are able to do in this life without knowing how we do it, something which is granted to every believer.

Learn to pray more every day, to become, at the feet of Jesus Christ, an inhabitant of that small city of which Abraham spoke in Genesis: My town is a small one and there will I live, it is quite small and there my soul finds its life. Quite a small place, like that held by Thérèse of Lisieux, is as great as the world.

Your relationship with your family is the same as I myself experienced when I was a young man. Pray for them increasingly; they need your prayers and sacrifices all the time, by which others will certainly profit even if they fail to do so.

What a joy it is to spend the time from morning and evening with the truth, to possess this gift and only to have to open one's heart and one's hands in order to spread it around one. If only Christians could realize what hungry and desperate eyes surround them and are looking at them.

I am glad you see Isabelle Rivière so often. She is a real friend and will be a great help to you.

Give me some definite information about what you are doing and the career you have in mind. The prayer which I ask you to say for me is that the Will of God may be done above all and so clearly shown that my own may vanish.

Dear sister in Jesus Christ, I say to you: courage. And thanks.

P. Claudel

The quality of such a reply would be ruined by any commentary. Claudel was from the start taking to heart his role as guide. He knew I was isolated, and the horizons he was opening out before me corresponded to his own stature. How could I have failed to listen to him eagerly?

I followed up his letters with the progressive reading of his works: *Tête d'Or* (not always fully understood, I must admit), then *L'Otage* and finally the radiant *Annonce à Marie*.[1] All my holidays, as I wrote later to Claudel, were illuminated by his poetry.

One after the other, kindly and luminous, *Sygne* and *Violaine* were brought to me. Nowhere else had I come across such pure faces, unless perhaps those of Antigone and Beatrice. Where did the poet find his model? Could it have been Mary herself? Claudel often said that he did not try and picture a woman without having the Blessed Virgin, the Seat of Wis-

---

[1] *The Tidings Brought to Mary*. Published by Chatto & Windus.

dom, present to his mind as if in a mirror. In Violaine above all, who by her sacrifice carried on the work of the redemption which had been accepted by Mary at Nazareth, we can see a lowly but nevertheless very touching replica of the majestic Mother of God. She is indeed *consumed like the paschal candle, on a golden candlestick, in the midst of the choir for the glory of the Church.*

If we consider with what insistence Claudel took up and returned to this theme in *La jeune fille Violaine* and *L'Annonce faite à Marie*, and all the trouble he took to the very end of his life to have this play produced on the stage, it would seem abundantly clear that Violaine is his favorite dramatic character and that in her lies concealed the best part of his heart . . . he has engraved her fine profile with the genuine love of a father with all the resources of his genius and his soul.

It is in such art that we must seek the true Claudel, that which is best and most perfect. To those who are repelled by his rough exterior, we must point out that such delicacy could only be produced by a heart that was truly gentle and subtle, that only dared to reveal itself through the medium of poetry.

Years later, Daniel-Rops was to make the same remark. "This depth of feeling with which he was able to endow his most perfect heroines, was in the first place his own . . . but he concealed this depth of feeling from the eyes of men, knowing that the truth of the heart belongs to God alone."[1] *Only a heart that has been purified can understand the smell of a rose,*[2] he was to write later. We can be certain that he understood his own reticence.

In spite of being so far away, the poet thus began to show me much kindness—but it was not only along with his theater heroines that I was to enjoy his riches and his goodness. I was also to meet numbers of people, sometimes directly and other times indirectly, as the result of his influence. This was a providential blessing. I shall always place Isabelle Rivière first among these, and cannot wait longer before recalling her memory. She will forgive me if in any way I trespass on her modesty.

I went to see her the day after my first meeting with Claudel, in January, 1926, and told her as simply as I could about my conversion and my debt to her husband. There is no need to say that we became united by a deep sympathy. I often went to have a talk with her in the evenings, in Jacques' old office, where I used to sit on the same divan where he had breathed his last. In such surroundings touching memories were recalled, but I also received much valuable advice and encouragement from that soul brought to maturity by trials, and these were of the greatest help to a naive beginner.

I can never tell how great and how varied were the

---

[1] *Réponse à Wladimir d'Ormesson,* March 21, 1957.
[2] *L'Oiseau noir dans le soleil levant,* p. 127.

benefits I received through this delightful friendship.
Led by these two exceptional guides, Claudel and
Isabelle, I was able to follow the road before me with
absolute security.

God was not spoiling me *all* the time, however . . .
without asking for sacrifices. My parents were astonished at the rapid and profound change in my attitude
and opinions and found it hard to accept my breach
with Unbelief. Family life, which had up till then
been without a cloud, became definitely distressing.
Christ stood between us, the Cornerstone in whom
two ways of thought met. Though he was waiting
till later to give us magnificent compensation, for the
moment the cross which he placed between us, a
sign of contradiction, gave us much to suffer. On my
side I needed so much more understanding and sup-
pleness to soften the conflict. Youth too can be un-
yielding in its convictions and often wounds by its
hardness.

Claudel, who had been through a similar situation
in his youth, understood me. As will be seen, his
letters maintained my courage and gave me the confidence to persevere.

At the beginning of 1927 I received this moving
letter.

FRENCH EMBASSY TO JAPAN
Tokyo
December 10, 1926

My Dear,

My conscience troubles me because I have not answered

your letter before, but many things have been happening to me, among others my appointment to Washington. I am leaving Japan on the 11th (January) and will arrive there at the beginning of February; then to France at the end of March, for my eldest daughter's wedding.

Your letters always please me very much. The number of souls who love Jesus Christ is so small. My correspondence is usually with people who are half-dead and whom one attempts to bring to life. And in most cases, after months and years, there is no result to be seen.

Be a soul of flame!

Give yourself to the Savior of men without reserve or counting the cost, with the simplicity of a child and the courage of a lion.

Eternal happiness is holding its arms out wide to us. What have we to risk if we respond recklessly?

If there is a sacrifice to be made, do it with a song!

I am nearing the end of my life—how I regret that I have been dragging this load of literary nonsense behind me. How much better it would have been if I had given myself simply and completely, as I once tried to do. How I wish that before I come to die a few years might be set aside just for praying and loving.

In your case, you are young and have a long life before you, a great career of joy and doing good. You do not have to stumble along between divergent and badly marked roads. I envy you your happiness. You have only to go straight on, ever onwards, ever upwards, each day bringing you to a fresh discovery. Or if married life is your vocation, there again it is a matter of simple duty, which can be carried out without doubts and without remorse.

Tell Isabelle Rivière how much I look forward to seeing her again.

PAUL CLAUDEL

This fine letter did not consist of empty phrases.
We should notice first of all that punctuality in
answering which distinguished Claudel down to his
last days. He did not think that distance and diplomatic promotion were reasons for making excuses. In
the course of the thirty years during which our correspondence lasted, I never had to wait for a reply.
Sometimes it arrived sooner than I had expected.

Claudel made a point of not wearying the patience
of his correspondents, out of courtesy and above all
out of charity. Even less would he have left a letter
unanswered.

We must imagine what this sense of duty must
have meant to a man already overwhelmed by his
correspondence, which included letters of every kind,
literary, diplomatic, religious, from his family and
from his friends. He was only able to achieve this by
keeping to a strict rule of life. Every day he kept to
the time-table he had set for himself and was as faithful to it as a monk is to the bell summoning him to
Office.[1]

It was this absolute regularity of life which made
him so balanced, and also enabled him to take on
more work without being submerged. There was in
fact no dividing line between the discipline of his
time and that of his feelings, which has already been
mentioned; it was the complete self-control of a char-

[1] It is said that Claudel was so faithful to his daily time-table
that the baker at Brangues did not need to look at his clock, for
he saw him pass by every evening at five o'clock on his way to
church.

acter which could master itself on every occasion.

In spite of his astonishing literary output (more than eighty works), "never," so Wladimir d'Ormesson tells us, "was a poem allowed to come before an official dispatch."[1] His duties of state came first, followed by the others, each in its turn.

With the same exact and conscientious hand he could draw up a report on Chinese railways—or lightly trace in *Sentences for Fans*, those exquisite *Phrases pour éventails*—or reply to some leading statesman, to a man of letters or to some soul who had confided in him and whom he simply advised "to go straight on, ever onwards, ever upwards." He might, on the other hand, have before his eyes beautiful, deeply engrossing images—fire and heat, the lion and its courage.

In the spring of 1927, then, Claudel returned to Paris for the marriage of his daughter Marie. I went to see him soon afterwards, and he consented to sign a whole *pile* of his works!

I was also to meet him at certain literary gatherings and discussions to which he invited me; among others I remember one at which he read his poems and the Abbé Calvet proclaimed, rather with enthusiasm:

"Not only are you the Ambassador of France, you are the Ambassador of Poetry!"

During that year 1927, I had the happiness of meeting an eager follower of Claudel, in the person of Stanislas Fumet. I have the most delightful mem-

[1] Address on his admission to the Académie Française, March 21, 1957.

ories of hours spent with him and his wife, the charming Aniouta with hair like silver. Even if Claudel did not actually bring about this meeting, nevertheless he was the bond between us, and his name kept coming up in our conversations. When a visitor came to join that friendly little circle, Stanislas as he introduced me never failed to add, in his usual spontaneous way, "a friend of Claudel's." The coldest person could not withstand that magic word.

It was with the Fumets that I met Piet van der Meer, whom I was to see thirty years later in a Benedictine habit, as Sub-Prior of St. Paul's Abbey at Oosterhout, long after his marvelous adventure.

Thus there increased the number of noble and committed souls whom God sent as models and supports in the journey towards him. He had already made me feel the attraction of a consecrated life, but I was keeping this divine call a secret as I waited for a clear sign of my vocation. This sign came much more rapidly than I expected. This is how it happened.

One day I asked Stanislas for the address of a community with whom I could make a few days' retreat, and he suggested, without any idea of the new direction he was giving to a whole life, a certain religious house abroad. He worked out the cost of the journey for me and as the sum was not beyond my means, I crossed the frontier the following August. From the first, I was greatly attracted by the monastic atmosphere, by the welcome I was given and by the Offices . . . so much so, that when I returned home

I had, without being fully aware of the fact, left my heart behind me.

In the course of my return journey, I had a long wait on the way. A simple question from an unknown priest became the sign of an overwhelming call to the religious life.

God does not need special devices when he wants to speak to the depths of our hearts. A word, sometimes the most ordinary word, sometimes used without thinking, can awaken the most surprising echoes. We believe with absolute certainty that he has spoken.

Three roses laid at the foot of the altar were a sign of my acceptance.

On my return to Paris I found a letter waiting for me from Jacques Maritain, which invited me to attend a Thomist retreat at Meudon, given by Father Bernadot in a convent just by the Maritain house. The hours of recollection spent there did much to fortify my new vocation. By the end of the retreat it was definitely established. Indeed, in the deeply religious circle which the Maritains produced round them, how could such a vocation fail to find a favorable climate?

The retreat ended with a program of Thomistic studies, with talks by people of the first rank. It was a delight to hear the question of "sacramentalism" discussed by such writers and theologians as Charles Journet, Bruno Froissart, Jacques and Raïssa Maritain. I even had the good fortune to talk about my decision with Father Charles Heurion (who also happened to be at Meudon). I was given his blessing. Stanislas and Aniouta were also there, so I traveled back with them.

We said goodbye after we left the train at Montparnasse. Stanislas must have noticed an unusual expression on my face.

"Are you in love with somebody?" He seemed quite surprised, and it was his manner to be a little outspoken.

My only reply was a not-too-veiled look at his wife, who knew very well that I was in love.

4

THOSE I TRY TO HELP

IT WAS CHRIST I loved and I was soon to join him. Three months later I was knocking at the door of this convent which so attracted me. It all happened so rapidly that I took no time to say goodbye to my friends. A short time before, without being aware of quite how pointed her words were at the moment, Aniouta had said to me, "God takes people away just like the marriages of this world."

God had in fact taken me away from my country, my family and my friends, not without some heartbreak, especially that of my parents who were deeply distressed. I did not know till later, and was thus spared a great deal, that the blow nearly proved fatal for my mother, who asked me not to write to her any more lest I should open up again a wound she found too painful. This silence lasted for four and a half years, after which "he who had taken me away" compensated magnificently for the sacrifice for which he had asked. All this time I was answering a call which I could not resist, and in spite of my tears I would have gone through fire and water to do so.

What did Paul Claudel know of this? Nothing as yet. Things had happened too rapidly for me to keep him informed. So, he heard of my departure for Bruges, not from me, but from Isabelle Rivière.

This was the astonishing answer that I received from Washington, the way this formidable ambassador wrote to that little postulant.

FRENCH EMBASSY TO THE UNITED STATES
Washington
February 18, 1929

My dear Sister in Jesus Christ,

What wonderful and joyful news Isabelle Rivière sends me and how happy I am to have it confirmed by letter. How small I feel compared to you, for without turning this way and that you have been able to make the small, direct movement of giving yourself to our Lord in all simplicity.

For you the winter is over—the time of cold, of fog and rain, of everything which leads astray, which darkens and repels—and the spring has come, the sun shines constantly. For now you live face to face, your heart forever with your spouse. To you, yourself, was it said, "Come, bride of Christ, the time of departure has arrived, the voice of the Eternal Dove, the Holy Spirit, is to be heard . . . Leave your father's house, like Abraham in the old days. Listen, my daughter, and bow your head. Forget the house of your birth, because I myself, of whom the book of life speaks, I am here, *Ecce adsum.* The Master is here and has called you by name, and you will leave no more that place at his feet which is yours for all eternity."

If your superiors will allow you, I should like to have

some details of your house, of the reasons why you chose
it, of the life you live there and the work you have to do.
I have often thought that the Church will be saved by
women, and that when the Christian restoration takes
place, as one day it will, women will play the leading part.
I believe it is the case that your order leaves much liberty
for outside works, and that in this way you are well
adapted to modern life. I expect that adoration of the
Blessed Sacrament also holds a large place. Please let me
know about all this.

I am sorry to tell you that what you have to say about
your family applies also to my own . . . as for my aged
mother, who has been ill for a year with an incurable
disease, I have much difficulty in persuading her to make
an act of faith.

Almost at the same time as your letter I received dreadful news. A very dear friend, with whom I had for a long
time exchanged letters and who, from the depths of his
distressed soul was seeking for God, has committed suicide.
When I left for America he wished to travel with me as
far as Saint-Nazaire. For four hours I talked to him about
God. I shall never forget the look in his eyes, because I
should have asked him about himself. It is in circumstances of this sort that one realizes how much one lacks
by not being a priest.

With my respectful Greetings in Christ Jesus.

PAUL CLAUDEL

Pray for me, for my family and for all those I try to
help.

When did a postulant ever receive such a letter of
encouragement on entering a convent? I especially

appreciated the fine lyrical passage in which the poet with his thread of inspiration wove together the verses of the Song of Songs with those of the Psalms, of the Prophet Isaias and of the Gospels. It was for me to try and keep my life in religion up to the standard that had thus been set before me.

One of my first joys after that was to receive the religious habit on the actual date of Claudel's birthday, August 6th. Wasn't this further sign that God was blessing our friendship in a special way?

This is how the poet replied.

FRENCH EMBASSY TO UNITED STATES
Washington

SS. Peter and Paul, 1929

My dear Sister,

This is my feast day and this morning at Mass I was thinking of you all the time with a full heart, of you in your convent where you have carried my name and notice to the heart and ears of our Lord. What a joy and pride it was for me as well to think that my birthday has been chosen for your clothing with the habit, and that I have had the honor to contribute towards giving our Savior one of his brides.

When the time comes for me to go, I will be able to think that my life has not been completely useless.

I was most interested to have the details of your congregation, and I hope to be receiving many more. The Apostolate and the Liturgy. These are the formula for the future, and when I was in Japan there was brought home to me what results they could have in Asiatic countries. We do not need to go so far, however, for we can see in Europe, in Belgium and in France, how the simple telling of the Word of God has a power which we forget all too easily. It was that Word which converted me without my being fully aware what I was being told. Women will also have a great part to play. The age which lies before us will belong to them. I hope that your apostolate is not hampered by restrictive rules.

May I ask for your prayers for a highly intelligent and cultivated lady whom I am trying at this time to draw towards the faith, and also for my dear old mother who has just died at the age of ninety years. The prayers of forty years have, thanks be to God, been answered. It was granted to all of us that she should receive Extreme Unction and the Viaticum. I feel sure she is saved and that all is well.

Finally, we must pray for the souls of Rivière and his friends. Isabelle seldom sends me any news of herself but I know the strength and dignity with which she bears the burdens of widowhood.

I can, thank God, go to Mass each morning in a church dedicated to Saint Paul. What would become of me without this daily hour of complete immersion in the divine joy? How envious I am that you can give up your whole day to it, spending it in the radiance of the Blessed Sacrament.

I have more or less given up writing about secular things and for the last six months have been intent on the study of the Apocalypse.

Yours with respectful gratitude,

P. Claudel

We can see how the poet was watching my first steps in the religious life with an affectionate heart, and how happy he was to have guided me there.

His deep piety refreshed itself each day at the source of Living Water and there it became "immersed." The secret of all his strength, joy and radiance was to be found there. So many souls seeking God consciously or unconsciously, came to him, and asked questions about his faith, and received much help from his letters and his advice. The letters which he wrote to me at that time bear witness to an intensive apostolic activity.

His literary work, on the other hand, was from the year 1929 to take a special direction. The Scriptures, with their matchless riches, became a perennial and sole source of inspiration. The strange thing is that it was a layman, a printer, who started him on this course, though unaware of the great impulse he was giving to a genius. This printer had asked him to write a preface for a new edition of the *Apocalypse*, and though at the start he felt some alarm, he eventually felt drawn to make a profound study of this wonderful scriptural document. As can be imagined, it was not the first time that Claudel had opened a Bible. We know how on the actual evening of his conversion he had turned to the Scriptures, in which two special passages pointed out for him a way of life, the Gospel story of the pilgrims to Emmaus, where we see the risen Christ revealing their meaning to his two disciples, and the eighth chapter of the Book of Proverbs which, in a similar perspective, sings the praise of the

Divine Wisdom and the Blessed Virgin. From that time onward, Claudel had several times read right through the sacred books, more, probably, than the average priest. He had not however intended to produce a written commentary, but a chance occasion had now arisen for him to do just this.

"I was sixty years old," he wrote later in *I Love the Bible*,[1] "I had nothing on hand, I was completely finished with *l'Otage* and *le Soulier de Satin*. I knew that *Tête d'Or* had come to terms once and for all with *Ysé* and *Prouhèze* . . . it did not seem likely that anything but death could bring to an end this rash and passionate research" in the vast field of the Scriptures.

From that time onwards only the Word of God would draw from this Christian a fresh flowering of his genius. For the next twenty-five years the pen of this ardent seeker in biblical territory would make notes of his ceaseless labors day by day. When the pen fell from his hand, it was so that he might see the object of his labors face to face, in the garden of the Heavenly Father, where "the Alpha becomes entwined with the Omega."[2]

On August 6th, then, I received the religious habit. My prayers and those of the poet were united with equal fervor.

In September I received the following letter.

[1] *J'aime la Bible*, p. 10.
[2] *Ibid.*, p. 11.

FRENCH EMBASSY TO THE UNITED STATES

Washington

September 2, 1929

My dear Sister,

Alas! It is not the case. I have not been in The Hague.[1] I have had to spend the whole summer here, far away from my own people, and I shall not be in Europe until next year. If I should be able to get there, I will certainly go to see you.

I had great spiritual consolations on August 6th, my birthday, and I only remembered later that it was the day when you were to take the veil and had promised to pray for me. It is thus you whom I must thank.

How I envy you that in this way you have the power to advance along the way of perfection, with freedom and with joy, all the obstacles having been overcome. It is of you that it has been written, "The snare is broken now and we are safe." The time has come for you to set others free, to give them life and light. This will be the age of the apostolate of women.

I ask you for your prayers and for those of your community for a soul of good will who is, I hope, on the road to the faith. You have no idea what prejudices there are against Catholics in America.

This country is extremely Protestant and the atmosphere produced by such a mentality can be overpowering.[2] How I envy you in your paradise of prayers and bells.

Let me have news of you from time to time, and pray for me, for my family and *those I try to help.* With respectful greetings in our Lord,

P. CLAUDEL

[1] There was a rumor that he was in Holland.
[2] Most Protestants agree, nowadays.

I had to wait for a year, the length of my novitiate, before I saw my correspondent again. He came back to Europe in June, and my good wishes for his feast day, which had been sent to America, reached him at Brangues, as he told me in this letter.

CHATEAU DE BRANGUES
Morestel (Isére)
July 16, 1930
Feast of Our Lady of Mount Carmel

My dear Sister,

Your kind thought of June 20th has been sent on to me from Washington. I am spending some weeks in the country in the midst of my five children, a rare happiness in a family dispersed as we are.

Thank you for not forgetting me in the precious refuge which you have been able to find, after passing through such fire and water. I, knowing well what determined and, unfortunately, often successful resistance people are able to offer to grace, can only congratulate and envy you.

I am still working at my commentary on the Apocalypse, and this truly wonderful book continues to provide me with glimpses of treasures without price. But the work is far from finished and I shall need several years yet. I may be going to Belgium in September for the performance of my *Eumenides*. In that case I will do my best to visit you.

Today a little Japanese is entering religion in the Carmel at Cholet. Let us hope it will not be long before a house is founded in that most interesting country.

With respectful greetings in our Lord,

P. CLAUDEL

I had scarcely received this letter when it was announced that my three years' profession would take place on the following September 8. I let Claudel know immediately, adding—and I dared hope for it— how happy it would make me if he attended.

What a joy it was to receive a simple post card with these words: "Yes, dear Sister, I hope to be present at your profession on September 8th."

GENEROUS TO HIS OWN

WHEN THE DAY came, a visitor knocked at our door shortly before Mass. Paul Claudel himself. He had kept his word, making nothing of a full two days' trip just to be present when I took my vows. Not a relation, not a friend was to be seen in the empty church. Then again, his presence alone was enough to fill the whole nave. For me, he was the Ambassador of France, and all my family as well.

At his prie-dieu, which we placed on a red carpet, he followed attentively the smallest action of the ceremonies, in a booklet provided for the faithful. When he came out he even asked for permission to take it with him. Our spiritual director, in the course of his customary address, did not fail to thank him. "Of the graces which God has given you," he said to me, "above all others stands the influence of the great writer who is also a great apostle, the reading of whose works made such an impression on you, and who was ready, on this special day, to honor you by being present at your profession."

There was a most delightful gathering afterwards

and at this our dear diplomat showed his interest in our work and told us about his labors on Holy Scripture. He told us how, at the time of his conversion, the priest who heard his confession gave him for his penance to read a passage of the Bible for half-an-hour every day of his life. He carried this out with complete obedience. He added, "I bless that man for giving me such a penance."

Now that the years have passed by, can we not in fact see that it was God himself who, by the voice of that priest, was leading him on to the most fruitful and valuable work of his whole life?

Later in the day, Claudel consented to read for us some of his poems. Those on Saint Benedict and Saint Scholastica met with our applause. "People say it is *impossible* to understand Claudel," he said with an impish smile.

A few photographs, affectionately kept, supplied our remembrances of a very happy day. We sent these on to him when he returned to America. This was his reply.

FRENCH EMBASSY, WASHINGTON
October 23, 1930

My dear Sister,

Thank you for your kind letter and all the charming reminders of a holy and radiant day. My mind still sees the charming crown formed around me by all you brides of Christ. Thanks also for the photographs, and for the lovely picture drawn especially for me.

He was writing in the same vein the following year:

July 20, 1931

I was greatly touched by your remembrance. I have
not lost the memory of that moving day when I saw you
coming forward with a candle in your hand to the altar
of the God who is "the giver of youth and happiness,"
and also the charming assembly, of nuns in white, in that
little cloister garden, while from all sides we could hear
the sound of bells. You have chosen the better part and
I hope that your parents are now reconciled with the
Eternal Plunderer.

On June 24th Copeau's daughter received the Benedictine habit and Jacqueline Rivière took her first vows.

I do not know if the bells bring you news of the world,
but never has it been in such a strange, critical and dis-
turbing state—not so much owing to external ills, as the
result of an almost incurable disorder in our currencies
and foreign exchange which is affecting all our economy.

The consoling thing is that nations can no longer live
in isolation and the misfortunes of one affect all the
others.

If only peoples, like individuals, could know "what is
the gift of God," instead of trusting to their own ideas
of justice, which are as confused as they are extravagant.

Remember me to all my good friends who are not
forgotten by me, and think sometimes of your distant
godfather when you receive Holy Communion.

P. CLAUDEL

With the intuition of a genius he had, a year beforehand, foreseen the financial collapse of the United
States in 1929, in spite of apparent prosperity, and in

the above letter, Claudel, with his finger on the pulse of the world, foresaw the disaster of 1939 in the economic disturbances of 1931. With the heart of a Christian, he suffered when he saw the world seeking for peace without God.

Nothing could be more charming than the letter, full of poetry, which he wrote me later when staying at Seven Springs Farm, not far from New York.

SEVEN SPRINGS FARM
Mount Kisco, New York
June 30, 1932

Dear Sister,

Today is the feast of my great patron, and I will make this an occasion to send you a few lines.

It is the most beautiful moment of summer and all around me, under a clear, fresh sky, nature is opening out with roses, honeysuckle, butterflies, fruits and young clusters of grapes . . . surpassing splendor, mysterious devotion! What a pity it is that the eyes and hearts of men do not open up more in the spirit of this ineffable song. There are, anyway, in the little gardens of a few convents some souls to whom God quietly explains his works and the support which he expects from them.

Thank you for still remembering my name and that of my daughter, whom I saw off yesterday on the way back to Paris.

With my most religious and affectionate remembrances to you and your companions,

P. CLAUDEL

The month of August, 1933, was an important

period for me. I found out that my family were at a seaside resort nearby, and then I had the great joy of hearing, merely by telephone call, that they were at last coming to visit me.

The happiness of seeing each other again, the powerful emotion which held us all, swept away in seconds the dark memory of those four endless years of silence. The whole community was in a state of rejoicing and the warmth of their welcome drove away tears and fears.

For my parents, and for all of us, this was a day never to be forgotten, so clearly was God at work. Such a *Magnificat* was sung that evening by the community, in which others were soon to join!

As can be imagined, I lost no time in passing on the news to my correspondent, all the more so now that he had been appointed Ambassador to Belgium, and it would be easier for us to exchange letters.

Claudel had already sent me a few lines promising that he would come to see me as soon as he was able.

In his letter of July 20, 1931, he had asked me to think of my "distant godfather." I reminded him of this and asked if I might address him in this way. On September 4, 1933, I received a letter from him which I found very charming.

CHATEAU DE BRANGUES
Morestel (Isère)

My dear Sister,

I share in your joy with all my heart, and the account

which you have given me of the return and reconciliation of your parents touched me a great deal. God is generous to his own and the courageous step which you took is now receiving its reward. By seeming to tread your natural feelings underfoot you have been the means of salvation to these three souls. I, who do much less, also obtain much less. There are souls for whom I have prayed with no success for thirty or forty years, my sister and her son for example, and my poor friend Berthelot (seriously ill at this time).

I am also much distressed about my daughter's future. Pray for her, I beg you.

I am sending you two copies of a little brochure which I had printed some time ago. Its only merit is that it will place before your eyes a number of the fine texts from Scripture which you already know and can certainly apply far better than I can.

I will indeed come and see you as soon as I can.

Meanwhile I agree with great pleasure and pride that you should call me your godfather. Did I not, in fact, lead you to the Feet of the Christ where you have found your home for all time?

In whom I ask you to accept my faithful and dutiful remembrance.

PAUL CLAUDEL

My novitiate was now drawing to its close and I was admitted to Solemn Vows on the following October 11. When I told him of this, though I did not ask him to do so, Claudel once again made the same gesture of sympathy and expressed a wish to be present. Besides this, my dear mother, who had been completely won over to my religious ideal, wrote to me on her return to Paris, "You have set us free, and our hearts are joyful and free of anxiety. Be happy then, and go forward with this beautiful life of calm and serenity. It is you who have chosen the better part."

It thus happened, at this most important moment of my life when I was about to commit myself forever to the service of the Lord, that these two who were dearest to me and whom I admired most became sureties for my vocation, which they surrounded with their encouragement and affection.

In spite of his wishes Claudel was unable to be present at the ceremony of my vows. At the last moment something official forced him to put off his visit till the next Sunday. This time there was nobody in the church, but my heart was full as I thought of my family who were now reconciled.

When I met Claudel in the parlor on the appointed day, he congratulated me with such joy and so insistently that I said to him with some surprise, "But, Godfather, you have converted so many others." In a very serious tone he answered, "Yes, but they have not all gone so far as this."

A conversation followed which I shall never forget. I found myself suddenly face to face with a poet in the full flood of inspiration, his wonderful biblical eloquence overflowing in waves.

He was working at that time on one of his finest commentaries on the Gospels, *A Poet Looks at the Cross.*[1] Filled with his subject he let me have some

[1] *Un poète regarde la croix.*

splendid flashes of genius, among others his meditation on the Seven Words of Christ.

These words, he said, are in the inverse order of those of the Our Father. While in the latter the first requests are to the Father and the last are concerned with men, on the cross Jesus turns first to men, then raises his eyes once again to his Father . . .

"*Sitio,* Jesus said . . . the life of the world is supposed to be well-balanced, but that of a believer is never well-balanced, because he thirsts. He reaches out towards something, towards God.

"There is a picture by Rubens which you probably know, his famous *Descent from the Cross.* It is very symbolical, very theological. Christ traverses it diagonally, one hand hanging down towards men, the other held out towards his Father. Up above the cross an old man and a young man are holding the shroud in their teeth. I see here a figure of the Old and the New Testament . . . the great spread-out shroud seems to flow from their mouths like a flood of prophecies . . . it is the Communion cloth on which we shall receive the Body of Christ. He is wrapped in this; the veil conceals and shows him forth at the same time. His own words are as it were a garment to him, as in the words of Psalm 103, *Amictus lumine sicut vestimento.* Christ is held in this, just as he is to be found from one end of the Scriptures to the other.

"What does the veil signify? In the Book of Proverbs it is said that *a vigorous wife will sell linen of her own weaving.* What is meant by selling? Exchanging

one form of enjoyment for a number of such forms.
I sell my cow, and for this I am able to buy not only
a cow, but a number of other things as well. Thus by
selling what we are we obtain something infinitely
greater, God himself.

"This piece of money is at the same time the yes,
and the circle which means zero, nothing. With that
nothing we buy Everything.

"The woman will sell the linen of which she has
deprived herself to the Canaanite, that is to say to
the old man.

"The same text says also that she will sell a girdle.
The girdle is that which fastens a garment round the
body, which adjusts it; she arranges the garment for
work, thus she expresses mortification, as Jesus laid it
down in the Gospels: *Sint lumbi vestri praecinti.* This
is adapted for each one of us just as the Scriptures
are for all. . . ."

Claudel spoke in this way, going straight ahead,
with a far-away look on his face as he pursued his
ideas. The words flowed on like some great river. I
sat quite still, for fear of interrupting this fine im-
promptu poem. I only regretted that I alone was there
to enjoy it.

He returned to the picture by Rubens.

"In the choice of colors there is also a hidden
meaning. At the foot of the cross, with her two hands
uplifted, Mary is in blue; blue stands for faith. Mary
Magdalene is on her knees, in green, this stands for

hope. Saint John, the ardent young man who is holding the ladder with one foot, and is preparing to go up, is in red; this stands for charity. Christ, in the middle, with one arm is touching the arm of the Heavenly Father, while his naked foot, on the opposite side, rests on the shoulder of the *sinful* woman."[1]

Somebody knocked at the door. It was Madame Claudel and her daughter Renée, to whom I was introduced. After a short conversation the visitors left, and I noted down carefully all his words, so that it is now possible for me to reproduce quite easily all that he said.

At that time I was giving courses in Latin to the novices and was carrying out some researches in the vocabulary of the Bible. My godfather, who always took an interest in my occupations, wrote to me on this subject.

"Your researches in the Latin vocabulary interest me very much. You would get some help from the Concordance published by Lethielleux. All the symbolism of the Middle Ages, which is really childish and based on insufficient knowledge, should be studied afresh with the detailed information which we have today. You should get your pupils to read the delightful *Moralia* of Saint Gregory." (Brussels, November 28, 1933.)

[1] This development of this commentary will be found in *Un poète regarde la croix*, pp. 97, 118, 203.

In 1934 I received two letters in which a paternal heart expressed itself in cheering words and little presents.

January 20, 1934

My dear Sister,

Tomorrow is the feast of Saint Agnes, and as a souvenir of your patron I am sending you a little picture by a painter who is partly Mexican and partly French, Jean Charlot. Also some little Chinese pictures.

Pray for me.

In the letter of good wishes which I sent him for the feast of Saint Paul I told him I was making a special effort to make progress in the spiritual life and not to disappoint him. I added these words: "Pray for me that people may say one day, there is a daughter worthy of Claudel, which means a true bride of Christ."

On July 1, he replied,

Thank you for your letter of good wishes which touched me greatly. There is, I know, something strong in you. It is calm, sure and ardent, and it gives me great happiness. There have been few clearer vocations than yours, and it seems that your good parents are becoming aware of this. After what you have told me, we may hope for everything. I join with you in praying for that intention, as you do so generously for mine.

Shortly I will send you two little books which I have just published and which may interest you.

My daughter and son-in-law will be touched by your

thoughts of them. They are founding a fine Christian family.[1]

Please accept my most devoted and faithful wishes in our Lord.

P. CLAUDEL

The following year, as Claudel's diplomatic career was nearing its end, he did not leave Belgium before he had paid me a short visit, accompanied by his son Pierre.[2]

In August, I received a little card from Brangues:

Thank you for your kind wishes. One more year on Claudel's shoulders. How happy I am to hear such really good news of your family. I pray and rejoice with you.

The Church is going through a time of great trials and great consolations.

I am with you whole-heartedly.

PAUL CLAUDEL

---

[1] He refers to his daughter Renée's marriage with Jacques Paris.
[2] February 10.

⟦6⟧

FIRST A PATRIARCH

THE "GOOD NEWS" I had shared with my godfather was my dear mother's impending return to the Church.

Her contact with the life of the convent had been the push back onto the road to God. Here was a person who, in her uprightness and delicacy, had been separated only in the externals. She was wonderfully receptive to Grace. In October, she made a second "First Communion" with real eagerness and renewed youth. The little flame which Claudel had lit in me was starting to spread, and, after God, he was the source of all the graces which flowered around me and constantly increased.

During a visit to Brussels, Claudel told me in these few lines how much he shared my joy.

1 SQUARE VAL-DE-LA-CAMBRE
Brussels
November 13, 1935

My dear Sister,

I am spending a few hours in Brussels, where I have been called to the bedside of a dying friend, and am using this opportunity to send you a few lines. It made me so happy to hear the good news which you give me of your mother's conversion, soon to be followed, I hope, by that of the rest of the family. Please continue to help me with your prayers.

I am now living in Paris at 11 rue Jean-Goujon.

With all my heart,

P. CLAUDEL

The following winter, while my mother was preparing for Confirmation, she felt it both a duty and a joy to pay a visit of gratitude to the man to whom indirectly she owed her soul. I was so happy at this meeting between the two people who had been such lights in my life, and who were now united through me in one religious bond. This meeting also made the reality of our link with Claudel that much deeper.

During the year which followed, our correspondence became rather spaced out. For one thing, in response to my mother's eagerness, my time was much taken up with her religious instruction. That was also the period when Claudel became very ill, and for a long while I had no news of him. From time to time a card from him assured me that I was not forgotten. Then came the war in 1939, which interrupted our correspondence till 1943.

This period of silence was far from sterile. I decided one day that I would get to know Claudel's latest works, which had been published just before the war and which I had not read as yet.

A boundless prospect of discovery opened to me.

These books were *The Sword and the Mirror, Figures and Parables, The Adventures of Sophie, Presence and Prophecy*[1] and others . . . some fifteen in all, most of them Scriptural commentaries which proved an unfailing source of help and pleasure.

It was really during this period that I first began to reach the depths of this wonderful work which both enriched my spiritual life and gave a new aspect, far deeper and more intimate, to our friendship.

At the beginning of 1943 I heard of certain facilities for correspondence recently granted with so-called free France, so I took the risk of writing to Claudel, whom I knew to be at Brangues. I told him how providentially we had been protected during the tornado of 1940 and asked for news of his family. Going on to tell him of my recent reading, I said how I hoped to make his writings better known by a little work which I proposed to write.

With great joy I received the reply soon afterwards.

CHATEAU DE BRANGUES
Morestel (Isère)
March 7, 1943

My dear Sister,

I was very pleased to receive your letter and to hear news of you after these years of terrible trial. Just as God has spared you, so has he spared my family and me, but

[1] *L'Epée et le Miroir, Figures et Paraboles, les Aventures de Sophie, Présence et Prophétie.*

three of my children are abroad and I have no means of making contact with them. My eldest daughter is in Paris and only the youngest, who was married three years ago and has just presented us with a lovely little grand-daughter, Marie-Victoire, is with us.

I now have fourteen grandchildren and there was a fifteenth who died. I really am, you can see, a patriarch. I am living on my property where, thanks to a little farm, we have never been short of anything.

All the good news which you give me of your convent and your activities interests me greatly. I hope that your town has not suffered in all that has happened to us.

You offer to send me a little picture. Do you know what would please me greatly? I admire your coif so much. I would be delighted to have a detailed sketch of it, both from the front, the back and in profile. This would be helpful to me in regard to a performance of *The Tidings Brought to Mary*, which the *Théâtre-Français* is putting on next winter. Who knows, you may even consent to explain it to the actress herself.

I hope your parents are well and have been spared in all that concerns them.

I am working regularly. I have completed an enormous book on the Apocalypse, and am now engaged on a kind of treatise on the Assumption. A few days ago I published a little booklet about prayer.[1]

Now that we are in contact once again, you must let me have news of you from time to time.

Please accept my respectful greetings.

P. CLAUDEL

I sent my correspondent the sketches he wanted,

---

[1] *Seigneur apprenez-nous à prier.*

and told him how I had started to write my little study of his work. To this he replied:

CHATEAU DE BRANGUES
Morestel (Isère)
May 29, 1943

My dear Sister,

I was delighted to get your letter of the 10th and also the drawings which you have made with such care, and which I hope we shall be able to use.[1]

All that you tell me about my books and the good which God allows them to do fills me with joy and gratitude. When we reach the end of life, it is good if we can feel it has not been useless. As regards the little book on prayer, there are some mistakes. The frontispiece should have the title Le *désert des chaises*,[2] and instead of *vers un Dieu*, towards a god, you should read *vers son Dieu*, towards one's God, or perhaps towards our God. Also, in Rembrandt's picture, I forgot to mention the cross, which is however outlined quite clearly.

I am busy at this time with some deeply interesting work, a commentary on the *Song of Songs*, and I am going ahead from discovery to discovery (in the most traditional sense). What a joy if I should be able to provide popular piety with this unrivaled poem. Most people can only see the husk, the literary beauty, and fail to understand the beauty that lies within.

I await with much interest the book you are writing about me. Since it seems that my work is doing some good, I of course hope to see it known and understood

[1] The performance of *L'Annonce faite à Marie* did not take place.
[2] The Desert of Chairs.

more and more. There is a time for sowing and a time for reaping.

I don't imagine you have a radio in your convent. That's a shame, for the other day you could have heard *Jeanne d'Arc au bûcher* directed by Honneger. A young Jesuit made a collection of extracts from my works, called *Pages de prose*, which will be appearing shortly.

I am, thanks be to God, always in the best of health, as are also my dear children from whom I am separated, and I only know that much about them.

Please give my best respects to your mother and my best wishes to your Prioress and your companions. Pray for me.

With all my heart, in those of the Savior and of Mary Immaculate. Oh yes, I have just written a short preface in regard to the miracles at Fatima.

P. CLAUDEL

Such a kind letter was a great encouragement. Besides, by the end of the summer, my little work was nearly finished. Though I had written it with a full heart, it had cost much trouble and effort. I was to know later with what graces it would be rewarded.

On October 19, 1943, I wrote a terribly long letter to Claudel. But he seemed very pleased with it. Here are a few extracts.

My dear Godfather,

Thank you very much indeed for your kind letter of May 29th, which I read with great pleasure. Before answering it, I waited till I had finished my little work, which I shall probably call *Claudel et la Liturgie*, and which I

humbly venture to dedicate to you. I shall be sending
it to you during the next four days, after making the
final corrections. I hope it reaches you safely. It is a piece
of work which has been carried out with joy and eagerness but without any literary object, with the sole aim
of making you more widely known. I have in fact broken
in two doors, both at the same time, the door that is
Claudel and the door of the Liturgy, both of which
needed to be broken in.

You will see, Godfather, how I have looked at your
work from a definitely religious standpoint, and that I
have tried, as I moved forward, to reveal the essential part
played by *La Muse qui est la Grâce*. We must discern
the contemplative in you, far more than the man of
letters. There are so many who do the contrary.

I am so much looking forward to hear what you think
of the title, of the sub-titles and especially of the third
part in which I have written of your spirituality. This is
certain to astonish more than one reader.

What do you think of this bringing together poetic
method and the three ways of the spiritual life? As for
the symbolism, I was fascinated by it. I found its basis
in these words, "I will tell you what each thing means."[1]
Every creature, in fact, has something to tell us, of which
the delicate leaves of your *Eventails*,[2] give us the secret.

. . . Godfather, what do you think of my vignette? I
have hopes that it may be a synthesis of your thought:
a prison bar removed, the water which brings freedom,
the rising star and the rose which sings.

. . . Finally, dear Godfather, I now venture to ask you
a serious question—would you be ready to give me the
great pleasure of contributing a few lines as a preface?
I know very well that the work does not deserve such an

[1] *Je vous dirai ce que chaque chose veut dire.*
[2] *Fans.*

honor, but I don't know how your fatherly heart could say no. Forgive my taking this liberty and may I hope for this from your kindness. Dom A. said to me on this subject, "It's a good idea. We may perhaps have something very interesting from Claudel on the liturgy."

I need hardly tell you how eagerly I am waiting for your reply, and I am grateful to you for it already.

I have been asked if you did not write *Le soulier d'or* (The Golden Shoe) or *Le pantoufle de vair* (The Vair[1] natively azure and argent. Bedroom Slipper)! There are always two or three who are especially interested and remain on at the end,[2] and they are, I think, really attracted when I read them some lines from your fine letters. I knew they would be appreciated. People write to me and want to read your works. Copies of these are almost impossible to find, so they lend each other books. What a circulation there is, they are so eager and devour all that they can get.

My mother is now becoming one of your apostles. She comforted a poor dying woman by reading her *The Sword*.[3] In my own case, I asked a very sick woman, whom I had persuaded to read your books, to tell me what effect they had on her. She replied, "This needs only one word. Claudel has taught me to say Yes." She has said to me many times, "I pray so much for Claudel. Thank him on my behalf. Without him, I would have had nothing to hold on to. I would not have been able to bear this illness." At this time we were reading *Présence et Prophétie*, especially the chapters on *Présence*, and *Sensation du divin*, but above all *La deuxième note sur les Anges*.[4]

[1] Vair is a heraldic term for small shield-shaped figures, alter-
[2] of her lectures on Claudel.
[3] *L'Epée*.
[4] Second Notes on the Angels.

They are dazzling, like fireworks. My soul seems to become liquified in the light, carried away on *that intellectual sea and that mathematical Paradise.*[1] I know whole pages by heart.

Dear Godfather, I'm embarassed by the length of this letter . . . I hope that you will soon visit us here and I will then be able to tell you many other things. Thank you for the strong, reassuring hand which you hold out to me. I shall never let go.

Be sure and tell me when I make mistakes, and if I have understood you. I only ask for that—to have understood you, and pleased you.

> Your grateful God-daughter

---

[1] *mer intellectuelle et ce Paradis mathématique.*

7

THE SATIN SLIPPER

D URING THIS PERIOD, preparations were being made in Paris for an event of the first magnitude in Claudel's life. They were about to produce *Le Soulier de Satin* at the *Théâtre-Français*. This was a very big undertaking, for there were adaptions to be made, and considerable research was necessary, as well as rich dresses and scenery. For a month beforehand the *Comédie* was in a state of feverish excitement, with producers, dress-designers, actors and musicians at work in all directions. However, as he himself said, "*The Satin Slipper* was the highest point of my artistic life, of which it was as it were the summary, while it was at the same time its conclusion."

A battalion of specialists of every kind were working without a break, day and night, to bring about a production which for twenty years had been considered impossible. Recast by Claudel, in collaboration with J-L. Barrault, it was under way on November 27, 1943. On this occasion the poet left his château at Brangues, entered the occupied zone, and followed the preparations on the spot.

He has described his emotion on the first night, and the joy he felt at seeing on the stage the play which he valued above all others, the synthesis of all his work for the theater.

The Satin Slipper had a wonderful success. The public showed the greatest eagerness and enthusiasm, and everywhere the remarkable *Slipper* was discussed . . . and the lyrical and religious powers of this masterpiece as well.

"People have rediscovered their need of greatness and eternity," wrote H. Lenormand in *Panorama*,[1] "their willingness for self-sacrifice, their desperate hope for Grace . . . it is by such inner shocks that the reality of a spiritual inheritance is asserted in hours of anguish and uncertainty."

We need only remember 1943, that period of the World War, so dark and uncertain for France and her allies. In the midst of those sad times when there seemed to be no hope, men and women like *Prouhèze* and *Rodrigo* sang of the joy of sacrificing themselves and of glorifying God. How many souls, even if we take into account a certain unavoidable snobbishness, must have drawn from this play fresh courage and a joyful hope? Will it ever be known what a beneficial role, as humanitarian as religious, Claudel played at that grave moment in the life of his country?

While the concentration camps were being filled, while the war was in full swing on all sides of the world, and humanity was learning in horror to what

[1] December 9, 1943.

depths of cruelty we can sink, Claudel's heroes and heroines showed to a broken and debased world not some classical stoicism but men and women of flesh and blood prepared to tear themselves from each other of their own free will, so that they might return transfigured, never more to be separated . . . in the kingdom of eternal love where all is peace and joy.

In the midst of this universal chaos, in the center of Europe, a woman at prayer was inviting souls to sing and was assigning them a meeting-place—not in prisons and concentration camps, but on a golden lake. For her, as for Joan at the stake, it was *the Joy which is the strongest—the Love which is the strongest* . . .

The poet was teaching a profound lesson at a providential time, no arid morality lecture, but a joyful impulse to reach the loftiest heights. Who knows that among the countless acts of bravery displayed by Paris and its population ten months later, at the time of their liberation, there were not here and there the sparks struck by *The Satin Slipper?*

"And now listen, *Monsieur le Public!* listen to *Madame l'Assistance*,"[2] wrote Claudel on the fiftieth appearance of the drama. "You will not go back without being affected by the play at which you have unwisely decided to be present. From behind this curtain which has been lowered, an appeal has been made to you. And without knowing it, you have been accompanied by someone who has heard it. Who has moved you, do you say? Yes, it is true,

[1] Listen to the audiences.

someone deep within you has moved you. *Medius vestri stetit quem vos nescitis.*"

Did not he who has stirred us, whom we know all too well for we have so often impeded his actions, during those evenings speak to hundreds of spectators?

As for me, a nun, far away, unknown to that public-without-number, and that crowd of actors . . . what part could I play in those performances which I would never see? I could only try and fulfill the duties of my state, and pray. Nothing would have been gained by success, unless the hearts of the public had been touched. And how could they be touched except by divine Grace, for which every Christian, every religious, wherever he may be, can beg, however dimly, by honest prayer.

This prayer issued spontaneously from my heart at the very moment when the curtain was rising on November 27. I wrote it down and here it is, its worth and its purpose here a testimony to the sheen of *The Satin Slipper*, which it quotes so often.

TO OUR LADY OF THE SATIN SLIPPER

Saturday
November 27, 1943, 5.30 p.m.
Eve of the 1st Sunday of Advent

*Come now, and free us, O Lord,
God of Power!*[1]

[1] Liturgical text for Advent which applies perfectly to the end of *The Satin Slipper*, "Deliverance for captive souls."

Lady of the Satin Slipper, at the moment when your daughters are about to sing of "the King who is to come,"[1] turn your eyes towards distant Paris from which a great and eager cry will rise this evening. Receive in your hands this Satin Slipper which your poet offers you. Bless every step of those who come this evening to hear and applaud.

Bless the forty actors and the fifty scene-shifters, the dress-makers and the decorators, the man who rings up the curtain, the program sellers, the girl in the box-office. Bless the least of those who, on this evening, will place a foot in this Slipper and will do something towards its success. May each one, down to the least important, the least aware of what is being achieved, be caught up by the wave of eager response which Rodriguo and Prouhèze and Dona Musica have come to spread among us.

May their hearts be awakened and their eyes be opened. May those above all who come to spend the hours there *listen* all the time. May they learn at the school of the Dona of the Seven Swords to hear the voice of the universe . . . *at the level of the waters . . . and become aware of the hidden music, the life, the songs, the words of love, the murmur of those numberless words that cannot be discerned. May they learn to be . . . the drop of water which forms part of the sea.* May they listen to the voice of guardian angels who would make them . . . *shining stars in the Spirit's breath.*

[1] Anthem for Matins, 1st Sunday of Advent.

May they hear Dona Musica when she . . . *gives them a meeting-place on a lake of gold . . .* and invites them to that *enchanted republic where souls pay each other visits on little boats for which one tear is sufficient ballast.* For, as she says of us, *it is not we who make the music, it is there already. Nothing of it is heard till we immerse ourselves with our ears covered.* May all those who have their eyes on her, *desire to sing and follow the measure which she imparts to them, in a low tone.*

Great saints of stone who from the bridge between heaven and earth come down from your pedestals, come to our spirits. You, James. Pilgrim of the West, lighthouse for two worlds, you who . . . *make our shells to flash in the rose-colored Atlantic*—teach us to lift our eyes toward you . . . *the great apostle of the firmament.*

You, Denis of Athens. Come, guide those who are wandering in the night with . . . *the lantern of your severed head, held high on the point of your hand.* You, too, Boniface. And Saint Ad-Libitum. Come to us, Hear us.

You, Good Angel, you who hold our hearts with a golden hook, see that they go not astray. Help us to *mend the broken rosary of the skies,* by giving us back the lost bead.

May all the buried, bound and immured feel their shackles breaking. May they be submerged by a great wave of eager response, so that the burning breath of heroism may set their hearts on fire, if not *per vias* rectas then *por linhas tortas* . . . should it not be by that which is simple in them, then by the manifold, the laborious and the intermingled; if it is not done in order, then let it be in disorder, but a disorder that will announce the trembling and the crumbling of the walls around them by which they are cut off from salvation. And in this time of trial, this valley of tears, may only one cry be heard:

Deliverance for captive souls.

8

TO DEVOUR ONE ANOTHER

M EANWHILE, what had happened to my manuscript?

I had given it to a trustworthy person who posted it in the North of France and sent it to my mother in Paris, where I knew that Claudel would be for the performances. His address had to be found, to catch him on the wing during his short stay in the capital. The weeks passed by but I received no acknowledgment. Had the parcel gone astray? I like to believe the simple fact was that some country squire was perusing its pages, in uniform, at a guard-post somewhere in France! Claudel was preparing to return to Brangues and my mother was distressed at not having received it.

It was almost the story of *Rodriguo* and his letter over again . . . but the angel of God who was holding our golden thread the whole time was not going to forsake us at such a moment. On the day before Claudel was due to leave Paris, the manuscript arrived at home.

Here is the account my mother gave me of this meeting.

"On December 2nd, at nine o'clock in the morning, I was received by Claudel in a fine house near the Etoile. He received me most kindly, with his hand held out, in a pleasant well-warmed study, and he especially asked me to thank you. There was something calm and serene about him. I told him about the 'little key'[1] and this made him smile. I returned home delighted with the charming welcome he had given me and pleased that I had no more cause for worry about your work. He 'would enjoy it at home,' said Claudel."

I felt it was an honor and a joy for me to learn that the great Claudel, in all the brilliance of his success, did not disdain the humble homage of his god-daughter. He gave her his sympathy even before he had read it. But, how would it be when he *had* read it?

Claudel was never known as a man easy to please, content with mediocrity.

On January 1, however, his reply came, and what a reply. In spite of the "Line of Demarcation,"[2] in spite of all imaginable obstacles, the preface I had hoped for was there, accompanied by a letter which pleased me immensely, as can be imagined . . .

[1] This was a reference to the Introduction.
[2] Separating occupied and unoccupied France.

Brangues
December 17, 1943

My *dear Sister,*

On my return from Paris, where *The Satin Slipper* received a welcome which, even in your cloister, you must have been able to catch the echoes, I was able to examine the manuscript which your mother had given me.

You have read me with so much heart, such application and such intelligence. How fortunate I am that my words should have the benefit, in order to attain their object, of a soul like yours. It is not enough to call your work an exact and penetrating study. It's a hymn! It is the praise and understanding of a brother by a sister. And as for me, my dear god-daughter, tell me why I may not have the simplicity to be pleased if I have been of help to you?

God guard you! Pray for me.

P. CLAUDEL

I was quite overwhelmed and I had to read the preface three times before I realized it was addressed to me. When he felt that he was understood, Claudel knew how to find words which he alone was able to use.

In my gratitude, I answered him on January 10.

Dear *Godfather,*

When I approached you for the first time, you wrote to me, "What a New Year present you are giving me." Eighteen years later, it is for me to say the same to you, and I do so with much confusion. I am well aware that

I am only able to find the most commonplace words to thank you for your great kindness to me.

That delightful letter in which your fatherly kindness shines out . . . the emotion of the poet who feels he is understood, *unde hoc mihi?* There are many who would envy me, were they to read those lines. As for the splendid preface, it is a diamond set in my little golden key, the "pebble of permanence" which will give my humble work a splendor it does not deserve. It is an honor I am not worthy of, but even more it is a joy. I never grow tired of meditating on the dazzling summary of the liturgical year which you have given us. One cannot fail to enjoy the *Opus Dei* (in its course throughout the year) even more, and to make the voice purer which "gives out love and truth" . . . In any case, I am abandoning that anonymity which I have jealously observed. She who was hiding herself in your shadow, you are now clothing with light.

My superiors and my sisters are all delighted and greatly appreciate what you have written, as do also our good brothers at Saint André. They have told me I am *spoilt*. That is true. It is enough to make dear M. pale with jealousy.

As for the performance of *The Satin Slipper*, need I tell you, dear Godfather, with what eager hearts we have followed it. Without being aware of the fact, I had offered my prayers on the day of November 27th for its success . . . and on the evening before, I learned that this happened to be the very date of your première. It was in a cloud of ardent zeal and prayer that your *Slipper* was carried up to heaven.

One of our sisters, a foreigner in the bargain and not one who understood you best, said to me in a tone full of admiration, "What is happening in Paris at this moment is worth more than winning a battle." The enclosed pages may give you an echo of that evening.

All that remained to do was to see to the publication of the book. This was unfortunately held up owing to the fact that, in that period of increasing shortages, paper was very scarce. I had to wait for two years before my book was able to appear.

As for Claudel, he answered with as much feeling and kindness as ever, on February 9.

Very dear Sister,

How can I thank you, and all your sisters with you, all that beautiful convent at Bruges, with the Superior at your head who has sent me such a charming card, for all your loyalty to Claudel, for all that mass of joyful energy and fervent prayer which you have placed at the feet of Our Lady of the Satin Slipper, and which has certainly made sure of the play's incredible success, a success which three months of almost uninterrupted performances has only served to increase.

People do not weary of it, and come three or four times, in spite of its length, in spite of having to queue, in spite of the inconvenient hour. And this with a Parisian public, and when the play which they applaud glorifies sacrifice, the sanctity of the vow and indissoluble marriage.

If the will of God had not been there, so many favorable elements would not have been brought together just when they were needed.

I am sending back to you the fine work which you have devoted to my liturgical efforts, and I am proud to have had this chance of writing an introduction. The longer I live the more I become aware of the harm and starvation which have been brought about by our neglect of the Scriptures and the Liturgy—which is in fact the Scriptures brought to life for our own day. There is no more urgent and necessary work than this, restoring them both to their place of honor. It is for that I am working, jointly with you.

For the last year, after finishing my work on the Apocalypse, I have been engrossed with the Song of Songs (I am just about to start on chapter six) and every day I am discovering fresh and fascinating lights. To think that we spend so much time on the pagan poets, while truly divine writings like these are left neglected, to gather dust.

After I have finished with the Song, I would like to make a free and easily understood translation of the Psalms—in the language of a French Christian of 1944! I have already translated the Gradual Psalms, and this has been published on behalf of an association for the paralyzed.

Praevalui adversus eum, I translate as "I have gotten the better of him."[1] "I have prevailed against him," *J'ai prévalu contre lui,* is to translate the Latin by the Greek.

Let me have news of you from time to time.

I think the prayer you have written is so beautiful that I should like to have it published in a review. Will you allow me to do this?

And now, my dear sister, blessed be our Lord Jesus Christ! Blessed be the Church! Blessed be the daughters of the Church![2] (They are the daughters of Jerusalem of the Song and of the Seventh Station.)

P. CLAUDEL

[1] The French is, *On l'a eu.*
[2] The French is, *Vive N.S. Jésus-Christ! Vive l'Église! Vivent les Filles de l'Église!* Most readers will agree that such exuberance presents a translation problem.

I replied that I would be very pleased for the prayer to be published, but I never heard what came of this. I was much taken up with the great dogmatic questions to be found in *The Satin Slipper*, so I made a little study of these and told Claudel in a note I sent him soon afterwards. He replied:

CHATEAU DE BRANGUES
Morestel-Brangues
May 3, 1944

Dear Mother Agnes,

I have received your exegesis of *The Satin Slipper* and I have read it with the keenest interest. It is a great happiness to be regarded in this way by the eyes of that Wisdom which the Scriptures tell us enters everywhere because it is so pure! I am impatiently waiting for the remainder which you have promised me. I have myself been guilty of an article which I allowed to be dragged from me against my will by the Swiss review *Formes et Couleurs* (which has given up a whole number to the *Slipper*). I insist above all on the highly complex and important role of Don Camillo, and of the role played by those whom the Scriptures call by various names, in order to reach the saints. Who needs the saints more than sinners? Between the commandment of God to love one another and that of nature to devour one another, there is a closer connection than we realize.

I have pointed this out in the new edition for the stage, which you may be able to obtain from Gallimard if you have it charged to me. What a fine and useful life you live. It is the blue and green Book of which Ruysbroeck speaks, all written in letters of gold, and it makes me very happy to know that my name appears here and there!

Please thank your director, and I have not forgotten his kind thoughts about me. My own thoughts often turn to Belgium and to all the cities of prayer which find a home there. May all the powers of prayer preserve us a *ventura ira!*

May our Lord and his most holy Mother bless you, you and your companions.

P. CLAUDEL

And then, one after the other, the occupied countries regained their liberty, France in August, Belgium in September. Families which had been scattered came together once again.

Shortly before all this happened I wrote to my godfather:

June 30, 1944

Very dear godfather,

On this your feastday it makes me happy to tell you how much I have thought of you and prayed for you, asking God to bless your work more and more, and to cause it to bear much fruit in souls.

Your views about Don Camillo have interested me greatly; his personality does not hold one's attention, because he is an unlikable man, but how necessary he is for the action of the play, by provoking the heroism of Prouhèze. Thank you very much for taking so much trouble over my pages about *The Slipper.* I am afraid that the continuation, sent on April 25th, has not reached you. If it does will you please let me know.

Today, St. Paul's, I received my contract for the book.
Three more months and it will be out. I have added to
it considerably since you read it, including a pen and ink
drawing which I made from a photograph taken here. I
hope you will not be displeased with it.

I hope you will soon be able to see your dear children
once again. *Gaudeamus.* There was some heavy bombing
on Pentecost Sunday, but otherwise all is quiet and calm
and we are full of hope.

Yours most affectionately in Xto.

In a later letter, written in February, I told Claudel
about the vicissitudes of our liberation. He replied . . .

Paris
HOTEL LANCASTER
7 Rue de Berri
March 13, 1945

My dear god-daughter,

I have received your letter of February, and was much
interested to hear of the conditions under which your
liberation took place. We must thank Divine Providence
by whom you were so clearly protected. As for me and
my nearest and dearest, it was the same with us and not
a hair was ruffled.

I am once again in touch with my children in England
and America, who have also come through unscathed.
My daughter in London may even spend the summer
with us and bring her children.

The Satin Slipper is still played from time to time,
always with great success. On Saturday they are having
a "poetry matinée" of my works, which is to be repeated

eight days later, this time with the addition of the first
fifty pages of the *Cantata*. This is a great, a strange and a
difficult experience. Finally, it is almost certain that next
autumn there will be a performance of *Le Père humilié*
at the Mathurins, with a remarkably good Spanish actress,
Maria Casarès. I made certain alterations in the text,
placing a heart in the place of the severed head!

The public seems to become even more keenly interested in all this, and I trust to your prayers so that some
good may come of it. Peace seems to be slowly drawing
nearer, but with it there also approaches from the East
the somber Giant who has already laid his foot on poor
Poland. You must pray for Poland, for Europe, for
France and for your godfather who, while he has much
to make him happy, has at the same time quite a lot of
worries.

As for you, I pray for God to protect you.

P. CLAUDEL

In September 1945, Brussels announced that *The
Satin Slipper* would be given at the *Théâtre de la
Monnaie*. This was a great event, for the entire cast
of the *Comédie-Française* had agreed to go. A special
train was engaged to take the actors and the baggage,
while a number of lorries were to carry the décor for
some thirty scenes. There were to be only two performances and seats soon became unobtainable, even
for the most skilled theatergoers.

It is necessary to read the notices which appeared
in the papers the next day to get an idea of the crowds
which beset the doors. It is true that Claudel was
there himself, and received a really wonderful ovation.
The old poet, now in his seventies, was at last winning

the public's favor. His message, which had forged its way in obscurity throughout a long life, was at last meeting with an enthusiastic echo. Brussels did not fall behind Paris in the marks of admiration and affection which it rendered to a poet whom it had revered for many years.

9

BELL IN THE CHURCH TOWER

THE DOORS of a convent are not so tightly locked and unassailable that such burning winds of enthusiasm cannot find a way past them.

Within my cloister, I shared with all my heart in this triumph. Besides, how could I fail to hear of such things, when from all sides my friends and those who had been to my lectures, knowing that I was "Claudel's god-daughter," were careful to let me know about the success of my great godfather? Many people came for me to tell them the story of how we had met, and they seemed to go away happy and strengthened. On my side, it was a joy to pass on the little flame and to introduce them to work that was at the same time so helpful and so sane. The young, in particular, showed great eagerness. I can remember, among others, two university students, both fanatical followers of Claudel, who went away even worse! The encounter I remember best was with an unknown lady who had resolved to see *Le Soulier de Satin* at any cost and thought she had a flash of genius when she came and asked me to get her a seat at *La Monnaie.* How

77

this made me laugh, though I expressed my regret that I did not have quite such wide influence. However, I gave her all the encouragement I could, and promised her my prayers for success.

The next week, she was back—her face radiant. "I have seen it," she exulted, "I saw *The Satin Slipper!*" This had been no easy achievement: there was a large crowd at the booking-office, but at this point somebody offered her a ticket. Then the doorman informed her that it was dated the day *before*. She was crushed, and she had been cheated. But when a woman wants something . . . the curtain had already risen; the young *Jesuit priest* had begun his opening speech. My obstinate friend did not lose her patience, and after half-an-hour she had worn down the ticket-collector's, and was able to work her way in among the standees.

The adventure ended with my being offered a magnificent copy of *Dodoitzu* (some really lovely poems by Claudel in the Japanese style, most attractively illustrated) by this unknown but delighted lady.

This simple little story shows what a high place Claudel found in the minds and hearts of the Belgians, and explains their enthusiasm on each occasion that he visited their country.

I need not say that as soon as I heard of his journey to Brussels I asked if he would come and see me. After ten years of absence, during which so much had taken place in the world, and also after the deeper knowledge I had gained of Claudel's works, I felt a

real need to meet him once again. He was however
snowed under with all kinds of obligations, and had
to explain that for the moment he could not do what
I asked. All the time I knew, however, that he would
keep a day for me when he had less to bother him.

So, I asked him once again, in a rather pushy way,
and got *quite* a reply.

FRENCH EMBASSY TO BELGIUM
September 26, 1945

My dear Sister,

Your letter makes me shudder! If I was so foolish as
to go to see you, nothing less than the fate of Orpheus
would be in store for me. You forget that I am 78 years
old! I must also put off my visit till I have less to do.
Tomorrow I absolutely must return to Paris, in order to
benefit from the ride which my friend Burgère has offered
me.

You accuse me of coldness and indifference towards
you and my friends. But do not forget that old men are
fragile creatures who must be handled carefully!

Le Soulier has been magnificently rendered to an enthusiastic audience. Your prayers have been heard indeed!

With all my heart,

P. CLAUDEL

I apologized most contritely for having annoyed
him. On his side he apologized to me for having
written a little harshly; this letter of October 27,
written from Brangues, touched me very much, and
showed me how a man of the world like he was, who
had received many honors, could yet preserve genuine

Christian humility. And yet, when his friends became too eager and exacting, he had to protect himself, to take up a distant attitude and sometimes be deliberately rough.

Without such severe self-discipline, a nature like his, which could easily overflow, would have squandered its gifts, gifts which came to him from God and which he had no right to dissipate.

Those who were offended by this occasional gruffness, by the cold or absent manner which he was likely to assume at ordinary gatherings (he would also use the excuse of deafness to avoid pointless conversations), often had no idea of the effort, of the ascetic determination, which this attitude used to cost him. He bore on his shoulders the weight of an unusual genius, only understood by a small number of people, among whom there was nobody great enough to stand alongside him. With that luminous intelligence and vivid, flashing imagination, he had a terrible sense of being *alone* . . . in a domain where nobody could reach him, and where for so long, he could reach out to nobody.

Claudel spent most of his life in such isolation, hemmed in by outstanding and unique gifts. This, I think, is how God quietly humbles the mighty, his way of counterbalancing the gift of genius. Claudel accepted the yoke, even if it galled him. Where he could have grown infatuated with his own superiority, he was in fact crushed by it. He was, knowingly, humbled beneath its weight, brought to nothing in the face of this singular gift of God . . .

It seems to me that the buffoonery and the jokes with which he would break out at the most unexpected times, even in some pathetic moments of his plays, constituted a necessary form of very personal relief, a means by which he could come down from his solemn pedestal, and enjoy himself, all of a sudden, and be like everybody else, just for a moment.

It is of course difficult to apply him to our standards and our way of seeing things. He was Paul Claudel from head to foot and we must be content with that.

I was completely convinced of this (though perhaps not as much as I am now!) but how could a daughter not want to see her father, and such a father?

Here is the October 27 letter, which should help understand his reason for refusing. I might add that when he made his next visit to Brussels, I repeated the invitation . . . and with the same lack of success!

CHATEAU DE BRANGES
Morestel-Brangues
October 27, 1945

My dear Sister,

Your letter fills me with remorse, for I feel I have grieved you by refusing to come to see you, and I must admit that I was afraid of all the eager affection of those who were awaiting me.

The very worldliness of Brussels seemed less exacting

and formidable for those inner reserves which a man of my age is bound to use economically.

Have I not already given you the best of me in my books? The little pictures are charming and I am going to slip them in between the pages of the books I use every day.

I am returning to you, written in my own hand, the two sentences which you suggested to me.

May God bless you.

And from Brussels, on the occasion of the performance of *Jeanne au bûcher:*

HOTEL METROPOLE
Brussels
February 3, 1946

Alas! my dear god-daughter, when I come to Belgium, all my time gets taken up and is indeed booked a long time beforehand, so that it is impossible for me to give you a whole day. You must forgive me.

The performance of *Jeanne* yesterday was a splendid one, overwhelming, except for the prologue, which misfired. I am awaiting the book with the deepest interest.

With all my heart,

PAUL CLAUDEL

The book, the precious book, was at last ready for publication; my first homage, as can be expected, was made to its subject, and this brought me the following.

CHATEAU DE BRANGUES
Morestel-Brangues
February 24, 1946

My dear Sister,

Once again, please forgive me for a number of things. I know how you want me to come to Bruges, but for a long time you have had the constant company of my books, which you understand so well, of my soul and of my thought, and my "rude bodily intervention,"[1] as Don Camillo says, would only cause a disturbance.

I have duly received your book and I had begun to read it with delight, but unfortunately my wife placed it among some books which I had decided to leave in Paris, and I shall not be able to finish it till I get back.

It will no doubt be said that you are too attached to this elderly P.C., but I know well that you only love God and Holy Church through him. That is my only merit. Bloy and Péguy were also servants of God. You have understood, however, that in my case I only found God through the Church. My last book on *The Song of Songs* is no more than an extolling of that sublime being, united as it is with the soul, with the Divine Wisdom and with the Blessed Virgin. My next book, *The Rose and the Rosary* (a collection of fragments which will shortly be published in Fribourg by Egloff), is also dedicated to the Church.

I read extracts from this when I lectured in Brussels. In Paris, at the *Institut Catholique*, I read my long *Introduction to the Apocalypse*, which will also be published in Fribourg. There was a very large audience.

In May, *Le Pere humilié* is to appear at the *Théâtre des*

---

[1] *Grossière intervention corporelle.*

Champs-Elysées—have I sent you this version? I am rely-
ing on your prayers as I did for *Satin Slipper*. You have no
doubt received the *Seven Psalms*. They have been well
translated into every language: why should I not translate
them into Claudelian? An essay has been published in
Paris by Plon on the Book of Job. Unfortunately this
number of *The Pleiads* is rather dear, 450 French francs.

And now you have heard all about my efforts. Thanks
to truly providential circumstances (a young convert
Jewess has let me have her flat, left vacant by her parents
who were massacred), I have been able to find quarters
in Paris, facing the Bois de Boulogne, and I shall install
myself there in the autumn.

May the good God bless you—yourself, your companions and your chaplain.

My respects to your mother.

P. CLAUDEL

This letter was a great comfort to me, for I knew
well that the picture brought to his mind by Don
Camillo would not prevent him from complying
with my dearest wish. I was also deeply touched by
the way in which the poet welcomed my essay for the
second time, especially by the charming way in which
he spoke about it. Claudel was far from sentimental,
but when he wished to express his affection he knew
how to do so with marked delicacy.

Very expressive of this were the various inscriptions
he would place in the books he gave to his friends,
accompanied by "most affectionately," or "in affectionate homage." I myself received from him at least

fifteen works inscribed in this way! At a later date, "for my dear god-child, on her birthday," and then the last ones of all, shorter and shorter, but deeply touching, "to Sister A, from her old friend." As the years passed by, the writing, which used to be so firm, became more and more shaky. But, in proportion, the heart became ever more confident.

At the time of which I write, as Claudel used to tell on himself, he had sent me a copy of *The Seven Penitential Psalms*, but unfortunately with an inscription he had intended for a priest, who no doubt received (at least so I thought) the one intended for me!

I told Claudel about this and sent with my letter one of the little sketches in which he took an expert interest and which always seemed to amuse him. One of these was suggested by a photograph taken without his knowing it in the church at Brangues. Claudel was to be seen hidden in a stall, head in hands, deeply concentrated in prayer.

The things which amused him were the props, in the foreground his broad-brimmed hat and short cudgel.

The reply I received was not without humor.

CHATEAU DE BRANGUES
Morestel-Brangues
March 6, 1946

My dear Sister,

First of all, please forgive me for the mistake I made.

I become more and more an idiot as I grow older. The Abbé Cyvoct is parish priest of Pierre-Chatel (Isère). I have written asking him to send you your copy which he must have in his possession. I am glad that this translation into Claudelian has not upset you too much. The preface explains what I have tried to do. It is the fashion to accuse the Psalms of ferocity, of Judaism, of materialism, etc. This is not my idea at all. I find in them only the language of God. I am glad to hear that M. le Chanoine H. approves, but my lecture to the *Institut Catholique de Paris* on the Apocalypse has had an even greater success. It was crowded out and seems to have made a deep impression.

I am still holding a grudge against my wife for taking your lovely book away from me, in which I can see that your whole soul is reaching out towards someone else even more than towards me. When I see you on one of my next journeys, we will have time to talk about all that.

Your liturgical apostolate is much needed. Would you *believe* that there are priests in Paris who now say Mass . . . *in French!!*

And what do you think of the new translation with which they are going to replace the Vulgate?

Your little drawing amused me very much. It is astonishing how you have been able to catch my silhouette. My children will be most amused with it. You have my hat and my stick right enough. The stick makes itself very useful to me as I am rather broken-winded, and the church is a long way off.

May God bless you, my very dear sister, you yourself, your companions and your dear mother.

P. CLAUDEL

This letter was very pleasing to me for more than

one reason. His visit was beginning to look more certain. The little drawings seemed to have appealed to Claudel and the thoughts which they aroused were well worth the effort they had entailed: Claudel spoke in such a sympathetic way of that hat and that stick—with such respect indeed, the respect which he felt for the good things God had placed at his disposal. His Christianity could be seen even in little things like that, for he would never have taken up a casual attitude towards such humble servants . . . They helped him get to church.

For himself he used the most unexpected epithets, "idiot . . . broken-winded." Once again, we see there the real Claudel, exactly as he was. In the same way, when he told of the crowds who flocked to hear him, he clearly did not do so in order to assert himself. Quite the contrary. This man who for sixty years had been writing without "literary success," enjoyed a certain happy astonishment of the simplest kind, absolutely different from the supercilious disdain of the author who has made his mark and grown blasé.

I sent him at once two more copies of *Claudel and the Liturgy*, for which he thanked me in the most charming manner. This also brought from him a beautiful lyrical flight, in which we find once more the Claudel of the *Grandes Odes* and in which *The Muse which is Grace* made the great bell of his catholic soul ring out, singing of the triumph of Christ for all the world to hear.

It is certainly one of the finest letters I received
from the poet.

CHATEAU DE BRANGUES
Morestel-Brangues
March 21, 1946

My dear Sister,

All these mishaps have had a happy result. I have
for the first time been able to read your work in quiet
circumstances and with my mind at rest. Your enthusiasm
has a freshness and a quality about it which does me
good. We need hearts and ears like yours, listening in-
tently so that they may fully perceive what one has to
say, what Another has perhaps used one in order to say.

You put it so well. It was the liturgy by the voice of
the Virgin which enlisted me in the service of God.
It taught me everything and inspired me in every way.

I am not a monk in choir but I am the bell in the
church tower, drawing men indefatigably,[1] calling the
whole world to the service of God, the whole of heaven,
of nature, of humanity, the whole universe!

I am the big bell in the midst of the universe, which,
as one of my poems tells, has sat down at table.

There is not one single peal, like that melancholy call
to attention, that endeavor without hope, which rings
out from time to time in Buddhist monasteries, as if in
order to make the vacuum even more vacant. It is an
all-powerful tide, wave upon wave, which over-runs and
submerges everything!

May God bless you.

[1] The phrase used by Claudel, *puisant inépuisablement,* cannot
be adequately translated into English in this context, in order to
give the play on the words.

My best wishes to your Sisters and all my friends in Bruges.

P. CLAUDEL

I expect you know that Brussels radio are to give *Le Festin de la Sagesse* at 8 o'clock tomorrow. This did not quite satisfy me in Paris.

It was amid the Alleluias of Holy Saturday that I read this letter, as I told Claudel in my letter of May 21.

I told him how my book had been read as far away as Martinique, whence a Créole friend, a former companion of Sorbonne days, wrote to me, "I read these passages of your book looking out on a countryside flooded with light, in which the palms, the bamboos and the red Cayenne roses were all joined together in the same act of rejoicing. And the joy of Easter was everywhere." The air-mail letter bore the Cayenne postmark. Was this not the place where *Deliverance for captive souls* should be sung?

On the following August 6 I received a very fine photograph which Claudel had cut out from a review. It had been taken at the *Théâtre des Champs-Elysées,* during a rehearsal of *Le Père humilie.* What a lively and sympathetic face he had, wide-awake, attentive, smiling, happy, kindly. Arriving on that day it was as if he were to say, "My dear daughter, you are sure to be thinking of your godfather's birthday, and here he is."

During the course of September a company of amateurs wished to produce *The Tidings Brought to Mary,* translated into Flemish at Ghent and asked Claudel if he would write a few lines of introduction. He had no better idea than to give them my address, asking that I should write the commentary! I was at a loss how I should do this, but I set to work at once. In order to be sure that I did not misrepresent the poet, I sent my little article to him first of all. He replied . . .

Brangues
October 2, 1946

My dear Sister,

Many thanks for all the trouble you have taken over the program. Your commentary is perfect.

I definitely intend to visit Brussels at the beginning of December for the various receptions they are holding for me (also a lecture on the Apocalypse).

I will do my best to go and see you, if someone will give me a lift.

With my respectful compliments,

P. CLAUDEL

Once again a letter which gave me great joy, and with reason, for he was pleased with my commentary and the great visit was now certain.

We had no difficulty in finding friends in Brussels who were more than willing to bring the poet to see us. He fixed his visit for December 13.

FRENCH EMBASSY IN BELGIUM
Tuesday, December 10, 1946

My dear Sister,

All is now settled. Keeping to your time-table, I will arrive in Bruges, thanks to M.N.'s car, at 11 o'clock on Friday the 13th, and I shall be leaving again at about 4 p.m.

Respectful compliments,

P. CLAUDEL

10

YET NOTHING IS SAID

IN HIS OCTOBER 2 letter, Claudel mentioned "the various receptions they are holding for me" in Brussels. As they coincided with our visit, we might take a look at what happened.

If we turn to that period we shall find that in 1946 the *Académie Française* opened its doors to Claudel. His official reception was to take place in March 1947. In Belgium, where he had many followers, this distinction was widely applauded and Belgium, too, decided to offer him an academician's sword. A well-known journal, *l'Eventail*, opened a subscription list headed by Queen Elizabeth of the Belgians and Cardinal Van Roey. A Belgian artist, Marcel Woulfers, was chosen to design the sword.

The official presentation took place on December 10, in the *Palais des Académies*. Eminent Belgians and representatives of other countries were present, including the Cardinal and the nuncio, Archbishop Cento, and the whole diplomatic corps. When Claudel arrived he received a great ovation.

There were several speeches, after which the sword

was offered him by Dr. Herman Vos, the Minister of Education.

"This old man," Claudel said in his speech of thanks, "who of all the soils he touched has kept only one grain of sand in his shoe," was much moved by the symbol which Belgium was offering him, while France, with the fingers of skilled men "was at work . . . to transform him into a green olive tree." Belgium was "a country the color of the sun, the color of straw" of which, while still a child, he already had an idea in the garden at Villeneuve, as from a forked tree he looked out beyond the Northern plains, swept by the winds. It was a country where the churches, "armored in slate," speak to each other neither in French nor in Flemish but in the catholic language of love of God.

There was a second function in honor of the poet the next day, on the initiative of the *Grandes Conférences Catholiques*. Speeches were made by Count Carton de Wiart, a Minister of State, and Henri Guillemin.

The third day, which was by no means the least, took place at Louvain, where the university conferred the degree of Doctor, *honoris causa*. . . . In his opening speech the Dean of the Faculty of Letters, M. E. Lousse, compared the French poet to "some great oak of the Tardenois, which the tempest of the wars had failed to uproot, and which now puts out its green leaves above the fallen trunks."

Then came the turn of Charles de Trooz to praise

Claudel as "the confessor and the witness for unity," holding in his hands "no longer the satin slipper of Dona Prouhèze, but the whole globe, the whole mechanism of the world."

If, in celebrating the merits of Claudel who "combines the boldness of an Archangel with the strength of a French peasant," de Trooz chose the happiest and the most exact similes, even more striking was the praise he gave to Claudel the Apostle, Claudel who "is like the eagles as they sweep down on their prey," and to whom so many young people of our day owe their Christianity.

Finally, the Rector Magnificus of the University, Mgr. Van Waeyenbergh, spoke to the assembly as he presented the diploma. On this diploma, among all the praise, three words must have been especially dear to the man who received them: *Filius Ecclesiae amantissimus*, most loving son of the Church. This was true indeed, for he had been this with all his strength, with a devotion and fidelity which he never failed and which no other Catholic author has surpassed. "In my case, I only found God through the Church."[1] In all his work every word complies with her sovereign authority.[2]

[1] Letter of Feb. 24, 1946.

[2] Here are a few lines taken from this section of Louvain's diploma . . . Seeing that this remarkable man Paul Claudel, formerly the Ambassador of the French Republic to H.M. the King of the Belgians, a poet of great genius and a most loving son of the Church, has by his work succeeded in bringing honor and fame to the Catholic faith, that he has animated literature with a Catholic spirit, that he has brought fresh life to the theater in

In his reply, Claudel made use of new and original images, particularly when he spoke of the "sword hung at his side by his brethren of the North," to which had been added the precious diploma, "like some heraldic[1] shield, a sure passport to the world beyond the grave, so as to give him a spiritual panoply."

As for this Claudel, crowned with laurels, loaded with honors, ears filled with praise from the most prominent people in Belgium, whither would he now be directing his steps?

To this convent, where his god-daughter was waiting for him in silence. She only knew in a rather vague way that her godfather had been feted in Brussels, and she knew nothing of the laurels of Louvain. Neither was anything said about it during the day. Claudel said nothing and left in the evening without even mentioning the great manifestations of which he had been the object.

He was not dazed by glory, quite the contrary. The Claudel I saw on that day was the humblest, gentlest, most self-effacing man I have ever met.

He had the great gift of not allowing himself to be

France, exercising indeed a very great influence all over the world, that he is the greatest French writer of our time and the most eminent Christian man of letters, acting as the ambassador of the Word of Truth, that he has shed his light not only on believers, but on unbelievers as well, is worthy, on account of the excellence of his genius and the number of his works, to be decorated with the noble laurel wreath of letters, most especially in a Catholic university . . .

[1] Another pun on *vair*.

intoxicated by success and of always keeping his balance by having his eyes fixed on Someone so much greater, to whom he owed everything. Claudel, eyes fixed on God, immersed in his light, overwhelmed when faced with his majesty, and all this transparently clear—such was the man I had the rare happiness of beholding on that December 13.

On that morning, in thick fog, a car drew up at our door. It was Paul Claudel, brought by our friends. I took him to a parlor where I was able to talk to him without interruption for an hour and a half—an unusual privilege.

This was our farewell—and we both knew it—before his departure for eternity. This thought, although we did not own to it, gave our conversation a striking atmosphere of affection and confidence.

Naturally, we came to making a general survey of the situation. Twenty years had gone by since his first letter to me. I showed it to him. He held it in his hands and read it slowly, while I tried to recall inwardly all that had happened since then. Claudel gave it back to me, with emotion on both sides. Then I handed him the little bundle containing all his letters, which I had kept with so much care. "Why you even kept the envelopes," he said. I laid out the addresses on the table, with the Tokyo, Washington and Brangues postmarks.

He read through them once more, and all that had passed between us came back. We talked about his children and his grandchildren, most of whom were still in America.

He made one observation which delighted me. I was telling him that the townspeople thought I was a relation, a niece or cousin.

"Well, that's so," he interrupted, "you're my godchild."

We talked about *The Satin Slipper,* and I asked him if he remembered the prayer I had composed.

"To Our Lady of the Satin Slipper? Oh yes, I gave it to the entire cast."

"To Jean-Louis Barrault?"

"Yes. And to Marie Bell." He added, "By the way, do you have my translation of the psalms?"

"You did send it to me," I reminded him, "but on account of the mistaken inscriptions I sent it to the Abbé Cyvoct, so I no longer have it."

"Here," he said, "take your pen and write down everything I have written which is to appear in the next six months." He began to dictate: *The Eye Hears,*[1] *Saint Francis,* "illustrated by Sert," *The Rose and the Rosary, Introduction to the Apocalypse,* "a preface to the big book," *Radiant Faces,*[2] *The Book of Job, Translation of Gradual Psalms,*[3] "with a prayer for the paralyzed."

"*A Hundred Sentences for Fans,*" he continued.

"Yes, I know each one of them—all hundred," I said.

[1] *L'oeil écoute.*
[2] *Visages radieux.*
[3] *La Traduction des Psaumes graduels.*

"*Presence and Prophecy.*"

"Oh, I like that book so much."

Claudel seemed surprised. "Oh, really? It is one of the most difficult."

"Even so, it's my favorite . . . especially the second note about the angels. And that mathematical paradise!"

Claudel was clearly happy to find himself understood and appreciated. This had been the case less often than I thought. And yet, the day before at Louvain? Before that, however, he had known an arid desert of silence and lack of understanding.

He insisted on certain titles, notably on *The Rose and the Rosary* and *Introduction to the Apocalypse,* saying,

"This is very important. But they are large works of four or five hundred pages."

I knew what "very important" meant. These works were the fruit of profound meditation, and the echo of sublime contemplation.

"I am now specially occupied with the Blessed Virgin. All has not yet been said as to who she was. She was well above all that has been said. Do you remember the beautiful chapter eight of the Book of Proverbs, 'The Lord possessed me in the beginning of his ways . . . I was set up from eternity . . .' It is thanks to Mary that we have been saved, though that is secondary in regard to God, but it is above all thanks to her that the order willed by God has been restored, and that is even more important."

For a moment I found once more the inspired Claudel of earlier days. But he had passed the stage where eloquence still had a part to play. Now, it was more of a prayer, a state of wonder before the Immaculate Mother for whom he had vowed a love that knew no rival, and whose praises he was glad to sing before me, having devoted to her hundreds of pages of his books. I was conscious of a great volume of love as it flowed from the lips of this devout son of the Blessed Virgin, in the most simple sentences, following each other as if he was saying a Rosary, with the subdued enthusiasm of an old man who had viewed all things with serenity.

It was his serenity which struck me most, the peaceful ending of a life of struggle, of work and of prayer. Love had given him inner order and peace. He was satisfied and content before God, a strange thing to stress, but it is rare enough. If we turn to the delightful collection called *Visages radieux* and read the poem *Du côté de la défense*, we recognize some of the ways in which we are all apt to reproach God every day. Claudel had understood, however, that our God "asks for pardon with the rose."

There was no regret, no harshness or animosity in his voice, just an almost childish confidence, freely given.

These were precious and unforgettable moments for me. The true Claudel, "the other Claudel" as Daniel-Rops was to say later, was allowing his heart to speak of the things of God.

"Mary is the *Theotokos*," he continued enthusiastically, "but she is also *our mother*. And the Creator who owes to her the restoration of the universal order is *grateful to her!*"

He was silent for a moment.

"When we speak of Mary, we also speak of the human soul, to which the words of the Angel apply. It is also to us that he says, 'Hail, thou who art full of grace; the Lord is with thee; blessed art thou among women!' "

His eyes shone lovingly, and a happy smile lit up the old man's thin face. I looked at him for a moment. Surely, he had changed during the past eleven years, five of them years of war. He seemed so fragile, but the spirit within him was stronger than ever.

He went on, "The Blessed Virgin is the subject of a large work I am now undertaking."

He was probably referring to his big *Commentary on The Song of Songs*.

Old memories once again came to the fore. I ventured a question:

"Godfather, did you really enter the monastery at Ligugé in the old days?"

"Yes, but I was aware I would not be able to stay there. I went one day to the novices' oratory, and while I was there God made it clear to me that this was not my vocation. The answer was *No*. It was very hard. I had made such efforts to enter there! . . .

"It was after that I went through a great struggle . . ."

Claudel stopped for a moment and looked at me. I said nothing. "That was a struggle in which I nearly came to grief," he added with a laugh. Once again he was silent and gave me a questioning look. The desire to be straightforward, to make sure that I knew him as he really was and did not have too high an opinion of him, seemed to urge him on to run himself down and tell me about his struggle. I had no wish that he should humble himself by some confession. I was silent for a few moments, pretending I did not understand, and merely asked what year this happened.

"Between 1900 and 1905."

Dinner-time was drawing near so I left him. Our spiritual director ate with him.

When my meal was over I made haste to join our two guests, who had just finished dessert. Claudel talked with admiration of Rabanus Maurus, of Origen and about exegesis. He seemed pleased to meet someone interested in his favorite subjects.

I had brought some sheets of paper on which I asked him to put his signature, as I wanted to give these to some of his most devoted readers. I then produced my own copy of *Claudel and the Liturgy* and asked him to copy into it a quotation I had chosen from the *Grandes Odes*.

He took up my pen and began to write the first words, *Voici qu'avec cette mèche,* See how with this wick . . . Then he stopped, as he recognized the words and guessed the allusion.

"But I do not agree!" he exclaimed. "Just what are you getting me to say?" He put down the pen.

"Yes, yes, godfather . . . oh well, as you wish. But put a nought . . . that will make up the four *sous!*"

The poet took up the pen and obediently wrote out the whole sentence.[1] He wrote very carefully, calmly, while only the furrows on his forehead showed the effort of his thought.

When he saw how he had given way, the Canon said to him, "I admire your patience!"

He looked back with amusement over his spectacles.

"Oh, you know, one must *always* oblige *women.*"

They talked about *Jeanne au bûcher.*

"You have not heard it?" he asked me. "Not even recorded?"

"No."

"That is a pity," he answered, and then in a weak but moving voice he began to sing the last lines, *Personne n'a un plus grand amour que de donner sa vie pour ceux qu'il aime* . . . This is the greatest love a man can show, that he should lay down his life for his friends. It was an effort for the old man, so much so that the last words scarcely rose above a murmur. The faraway voice combined with that lively glance showed the control of his spirit over his body.

We got up and took our guest into the large room

[1] Voici qu'avec cette méche de quatre sous j'ai allumè autour de vous toutes les étoiles qui font à votre présence une garde inextinguible. See how with this wick worth four sous I have lighted up around you all the stars, forming around you a guard which cannot be extinguished.

where the community was waiting for him. He was as gentle and amenable as a child and seemed to enjoy being surrounded and having such a fuss made over him.

As he entered the room, all the sisters greeted him with the hymn *Adeste fideles*, which he had heard in Notre-Dame de Paris at the time of his conversion. We were within a few days of the sixtieth anniversary of that event: much moved by the attention paid to him, Claudel sat down in the armchair surrounded by palms which we had ready for him.

"Yes, that was in 1886," he said as he seated himself. He spoke next of his birth in '68 and added, "I have been present at the birth of the great nations— at that time, it was Japan. Then Germany in '71, and Italy . . . and now, what remains of these countries? One after the other has fallen. And as for Stalin . . . he will go like the others. Amid all these falls, the Church alone remains on her feet." He said the word Church in a most impressive way. He continued:

"We have recently seen the most horrible events happen, without precedent in history. I am at present reading a book by an Italian author who writes about the massacres of the Jews, especially in the Warsaw Ghetto, where a million and-a-half Jews were herded together, dying of hunger. The children scooped out holes under the walls and made their way into the city to exchange anything they had for food. The sentries referred to them as rats and killed them if they showed their heads out of their holes. How horrible treating children that way!"

Claudel's voice trembled, and I guessed that his words expressed his reaction as a grandfather. In fact, at once he went on to say, "I am thinking of my own, if they had done that to them."

"I think," he continued, "that we should have a great ceremony of expiation in the Church, or at least in Rome, for these massacres of the Jews. The whole of humanity owes expiation. I have written to Maritain asking him to suggest this idea to the Pope. This fact is something greater even than the destruction of Jerusalem . . . and yet nothing is said. And this massacre of the innocents . . . are they not martyrs?

"In every outrage against humanity, and even in all human affairs, there is always to be found a religious reason in a greater or lesser degree.

"At the base of all human struggles, of this I am certain, God is always to be found implicitly. In France today, for instance, what is it which separates one party from another? The idea of God. This idea is an impassable wall."

I asked him, "Godfather, is this why you wrote that beautiful letter to the Chief Rabbi of France?"

"Yes, but it was not intended for the public. It nearly got me into trouble . . . The Rabbi sent a very fine answer."

I was very eager for Claudel to speak about the Bible to the community, so I asked him,

"And as regards your work on the Apocalypse, how far has it gone?"

"I have been studying the symbolism . . . *everything* in the Scriptures has a symbol. It was said that Pius XII's encyclical[1] had me in mind. Not at all. The Fathers of the Church, Rabanus Maurus, Origen, and later Pascal have all spoken of the symbolism of the Scriptures.

"As for the Apocalypse, it gives the answer to many of the questions which are found in reading the Bible, especially in the Book of Job. The Book of Job seems to me of great importance. We are faced in it with the problem of evil, but in the end there is no reply from God. Job cries out, he almost blasphemes. But God gives him no solution.

"Where is it to be found? In the Apocalypse, in which the Word says, *Ego adsum.* The Cross is the answer, and Christ who allows himself to be placed upon it. 'It is I—be not afraid.' As for your cross, there I am upon it. It is the one answer, there is no other . . ."

"On the day of my conversion," the poet told us, "when I returned to Notre-Dame, I took with me a Protestant Bible which had been given to my sister by a German friend. I opened it and lighted on the episode of the pilgrims to Emmaus, where Christ explained to them the meaning of the Scriptures. The other page I opened to was chapter eight of the Book

[1] *Divino Afflante Spiritu,* 1943.

of Proverbs, to which I referred this morning, the verses telling of the Immaculate Conception. Since then I have never written about a woman without having these verses in mind. The Woman throughout the Scriptures is the Virgin. The Church, the human soul. To whom God says, *Veni, amica mea, formosa, immaculata* . . . and each of these terms tells of an advance."

Someone asked, "Can we say that there are historical allusions in the Apocalypse?"

"I think that only the *Letter to the Churches* can be said to have a historical sense . . . these letters would correspond to the various periods of history. By a kind of paradox, we would seem to have reached the age of Philadelphia, for there is so much hatred!

"There are four horses of different color representing war, death, lust and famine . . . Then the scarlet Woman—but also the Woman 'that wore the sun for her mantle,' travailing in great pain and pursued by the dragon. This is the Church in a state of perpetual fecundity. The Church has always been portrayed as a woman."

I asked, "And the Ark of the Covenant, where is it? Will it ever be found?"

"The Ark of the Covenant," answered Claudel, "is none other than the Virgin. Could anything be finer?

"As for Anti-Christ, I do not think this means one single person, but a succession of them: Antiochus, Nero, Hitler, Henry VIII, Elizabeth, Catherine of

Russia . . . Napoleon, if you like! It has rather more a collective meaning."

He then alluded to the outlook and the aims of our congregation, and added: "You do such fine work! because you are founded on the Scriptures. The text of the Scriptures has a value all its own when it is recited. I have, on so many occasions, met souls who had been touched by the text itself."

The time was passing. Our distinguished guest must soon set out on his return journey. Before he did that I was determined to express our thanks, and improvised a little speech based on two Latin words, both dear to the poet.

Magnificat, that is the word which comes to our lips spontaneously, godfather, on this day when you have done us the great favor of coming among us, so near too to the sixtieth anniversary of the great event at Notre-Dame.

Adeste, it was that invitation to the shepherds which you heard sung on that day: *Come!* And like the stars you answered, *Adsum!* Here I am.

Here I am, Lord, to speak of you to the world.

And throughout the insoluble labyrinth of your travels, you never ceased to proclaim the name of Christ to every people.

And then one day, twenty years ago, I made my way to you, and once again you said, *Adsum!* You took the hand which I held out to you and which I have never withdrawn. It is even finer, godfather, that you

have never let go. So much so that you were ready
to grant my request and here you are, *Adsum*, once
more! And all the stars lit by the *mèche de quatre
sous*[1] are also here to give your presence a light that
cannot be put out . . .

At the same time the Sisters sang an Easter sequence
of which he was very fond, *Salve festa dies*.

Claudel, as I had expected, was much touched by
this little scene and told me of his emotion in a low
voice. While I was thanking him for all that my
religious life owed to him, he answered quite simply,
"Well then, my life has been worth something."

A few photographs were taken, and then we asked
our guest to come and see a fine Gothic statue of the
Blessed Virgin, in a room near the church on the
other side of the courtyard. He got into the car, and
I found myself quite naturally following him. (I was
not exactly adverse to the little drive.) When we
reached our destination I got out first. As he placed
his foot on the ground, Claudel had a slight attack
of giddiness which made him lose his balance. I turned
rapidly to help him, and thus it happened that for
the space of a second I was holding in my hands the
great Claudel!

We went at once into the room where he spent
a long time admiring the beautiful 13th-century statue
from the Champagne country, which thus made it
his compatriot. He gazed at it with that same look

---

[1] Two-penny wick, an allusion to the incident in the parlor.

of wonder which he had that morning when he spoke about the Blessed Virgin, and said quietly, "How beautiful it is, and what a charming face."

At last the time came when he must leave.

"Perhaps you will come back again," I said, without much hope.

"Oh, it is very difficult to come as far as here," he answered.

I pressed his hand affectionately, "Thank you, god-father."

He got into the car, and as it started, Claudel turned towards me and raised his arms slightly, with a gesture of blessing. This was the last sight I was to have of him, so deep, so touching, so full of meaning.

Yes, godfather, all that you did for me can be summed up in one word, blessing. You blessed my youth with all its hesitations, you blessed my religious life which was a joy to you, you blessed my mind which you guided, nourished and enlightened. You blessed my spirit which you drew away from the dangers of the world and guided to that home of peace where it is certain not to die.

Blessing, the one word which from the time I first came to know your splendid work, sprang from my heart with a great impulse of gratitude.

Now you have left us. My heart was divided then between the joy of such a radiant day and the sorrow of that farewell which must, how well I knew it, be the last.

11

A TIME TO SPEAK

S OME DAYS LATER I sent a letter to our visitor, by then in Paris. I venture a few extracts.

December 19, 1946

Very dear godfather,

I should like to be the first to send you my good wishes for the coming feast-day, and to tell you how much my sisters and I hope to share in your act of thanksgiving. In the *Adeste* which we sing at midnight, we shall think of the guest who was willing to come all that way to be with us, and to rejoice our souls with his grand meditations on the Apocalypse.

Some of my sisters told me that when you finished, they wanted to ask for your patriarchal blessing.

As for myself, have I any need to tell you of my joy and gratitude, and the unforgettable memories I have of that day when you spoke to me with such kindness, humility and confidence.

If the Brussels public heard the words of Claudel, I heard the silence of a soul prostrate before God—just as I had guessed from his writings and of which I became aware—far surpassing all that his poetry had revealed to me. Thank you for this joy which you have given me,

something unique in my life. I know now the absolute
sincerity of your work and how to reply to those who
might have any doubts.

It was not necessary that you recall any further a period
of your life which you had the great humility to mention
briefly. Your actions were enough . . . and please believe
that nothing can alter the veneration and filial affection
I have for you . . .

Though your stay was so short, I have remembered
most carefully all that you said to me. May I tell you
of an impression I received? It seemed to me you had
recently experienced the overwhelming power of the
Divine Majesty.

The beautiful statue of the Blessed Virgin which you
admired so much, sends you her most *lovely* smile, the
smile of the land of Champagne. I should be surprised
if the oak which gave it birth did not have its roots at
Villeneuve!

In any case I often speak to her of my godfather . . .
shouldn't I say father? Isn't it so? May I give you that
noble and venerable name? And you will give me your
paternal blessing? . . .

A few days later Claudel answered her whom he
called for the first time his *dear daughter*. He did so
with such simplicity and told of the emotion which
he felt after his visit.

11 Boulevard Lannes (XVI)
December 26, 1946

I also, my dear sister, my dear daughter, received great
pleasure, deep feeling and spiritual help from my short
stay in your beautiful convent. I still have many things

to say to you, some of them very important. My books will have to convey these to you, on my behalf.

I become aware of all those souls who dwell in the heart of the divine will and who are united to my own by no other bond than their weight, like the planets. *Amor meus, pondus meus.*

And yours is one of those which cannot be forgotten. Please remember me very kindly to Abbé H.

As a Christmas present I cannot do better than send you this book which will, I hope, interest you.

Vive Jésus!

P. CLAUDEL

An Introduction to the Book of Ruth arrived at the same time as his letter. I could discern in it an even deeper knowledge of the Bible and an imposing panoramic view of the history of Israel, given with remarkable conciseness. Before I had time to thank him, a second letter from him arrived, acknowledging a little collection of our pictures and a baptismal certificate which had appealed to Claudel while he was with us.

11 Boulevard Lannes (XVI)
January 3, 1947

My very dear Sister,

I have received the charming pictures. They have arrived at just the right moment: I have in fact become the godfather of a little child which was actually born on Christmas night in very touching and almost miraculous circumstances.

I have sent you *Ruth*. I hope it has reached you.

Please give my respects to the Reverend Mother and to your sisters, and to you my best thoughts in Xto Jesu.

What you tell me in your letter is very moving.

P. CLAUDEL

I hastened a reply . . .

January 8, 1947

My good godfather,

I am quite overwhelmed—two delightful letters and a book which I shall value greatly. I am deeply touched. Many thanks.

To me also "something magnificent has happened,"[1] for my meeting with you twenty-one years ago has never ceased to amaze me. There are so many others, of far more interest than me, who deserve your attention.

I have already read with eagerness a good part of your *Introduction*. I imagine you, complete with ephod and breastplate,[2] striking with your scalpel at the heart of the Scriptures.

It seems to me that while your dramatic and poetic work has given rise to much comment, your exegesis has not on the other hand received the response it deserves (apart from some ridiculous carping by members of the literalist school). How much I should like, if I had the time at my disposal, to write a little commentary for these works of yours, or rather an *initiation*, as I have done for your poetic works as a whole.

I have a number of ideas in mind, but shall I ever carry them out?

Your summary of the history of Israel reminds me of the maps I used to make to introduce some of my pupils

[1] The allusion is to his words in his speech at Brussels.
[2] Vestments worn by Aaron in the Tabernacle in the wilderness.

to the study of the Bible, and on which I marked all
the journeys of the Jewish people from Noe to St. Paul.
When I read your *Introduction*, these maps came to life
and were covered with all the people you describe with
such delightful humor. Around them were those symbols
of the animals, that "living alphabet" which God uses
in order to speak to us. Between your fingers the whole
thing begins to move, cries out, bellows and bleats . . .
and we find ourselves transported into the jungle of the
dear Pråkriti! I believe you have watched this, as it takes
place, so thoroughly that you would also know, dear
Godfather, how to put a dragon into a jar *ad illudendum
ei!*

I shall ask my Superiors if they will have it read in the
refectory, so that all my sisters may enjoy it. Yesterday
your two fine speeches in Brussels were read to us. Of all
the Claudels I know, the one in this speech is perhaps
the most moving, a Claudel who brings peace and charity
with him.[1] No longer Paul of Tarsus, thunderstruck on
the road to Damascus, but the Seer of Patmos, pale and
white-haired, as he repeats *Filioli, diligite.* . . . It is the
green olive tree of the Apocalypse, or the branch carried
by Noe's dove from the great Ark of Creation, giving out
the oil of cheerfulness, the unction of charity, which
flows, splashes and spurts out from all your work, but
above all from your last messages and speeches . . .

Dear Godfather, I know that this visit has established
a deep contact between us; you are moved by the confidence which it has established in me. May you be
strengthened by this purely spiritual understanding. For
some time it has seemed that I no longer speak to you as
if on earth, but *in cœli . . . conversatio nostra in cœlis
est* . . . in that glory which hope lets us plan to enjoy
one day.

[1] Speech to students.

The normal state of my thoughts of you is that I am not looking *in futuro* but at a present that is realized already.

I am more and more convinced that this friendship has been brought about by God, and is for his glory— something sacred which we will only understand in the light of that glory.

On January 1st, when your letter arrived, I also heard from that poor agnostic lady I mentioned to you. Between the requests of that eager creature, my soul has been joyfully torn asunder. Is not my work to distribute what you give me . . . to be perhaps your little *Sept-Epées*, one who, in the shade, lights the stars, the little *mèche de quatre sous* at work? (She now has enough to live on for some time, as a father from S-A said to me with some malice!)

May God bless our fine friendship.

This period from 1946 to 1948 was almost overflowing with friendship, most fertile in correspondence. But an even greater grace than those which I have described was to light up those years in a very special way. It came to me from the same source, through that remarkable man.

Among the readers of my little book that agnostic lady mentioned in my letter had been most interested, and had sent me a few rather cautious lines on the subject. I had never seen her, but I learned that she had for a long time been seeking for God along a path which led to the church.

She eventually came to see me at the beginning of winter and asked to help her along the way towards Baptism and to prepare her for this.

I can truly say that, among the many gifts which I received through Claudel's friendship, this was a royal one which outweighed the others.

It is a very special joy to be God's instrument: to open up the luminous depths of truth for a soul seeking it, to quell the doubts of that soul with the supernatural riches of dogma, slowly but surely to appease its thirst for higher things, with the promises of inexhaustible treasures to be found in faith. It is an even deeper joy to lead that soul to the threshold of the Church. Once the way has been prepared, to present it, to answer for it and to assist as the waters of Baptism are poured at that marvelous transformation, the new birth of a child of God.

That Sacrament which in old days was known as the Sacrament of Illumination was not only for her whom I was presenting at the font. It was opening up fresh horizons before me in which my own Baptism took on a more vivid meaning, more closely connected with the experiences of life.

And there was between her who became my goddaughter and the great man whom I claimed as my godfather an unbroken affinity.

A little card on which Claudel had written for her, in his own hand, this line from the *Grandes Odes:* *O credo des choses invisibles, je vous accepte avec un cœur catholique,*[1] affirmed this spiritual affinity which would be extended some months later to several other adult members of that family whom God had blessed.

[1] *Oh credo of things invisible, I accept you with a catholic heart.*

Claudel's friendship had thus ever wider contacts. People talk of the wide influence of this poet, but it is to little facts like these that they should turn. Such wonderful things, unfortunately, take place in the deep places of the person, and only in Heaven will the career of good deeds and of giving light which that great Christian had followed be fully known.

[12]

FIELD OF FRESH PAPER

ALL THIS TIME, a sensational event was in preparation in Paris, Claudel's official reception into the *Académie Française*. This took place, as we know, on March 13, 1947. There had been an idea it would never take place, so people wrote . . . It goes without saying that this reception added nothing to Claudel's reputation, but the gesture counted for much. To be made a member of the *Académie* meant that France gave her assent to the best in a literary tradition as rich as it is varied.[1] "This is not a man but a star," it was said.[2]

On the great day, "Never had so many been seen round the dome. The crush was suffocating. Green hats, green turbans, green scarves. The ladies were in the majority, along with very young people, and the priests, the number of priests . . . there was a Dominican and a monk in brown, and some in black, black without bands, without silver buckles . . .

". . . But here was Claudel with all his strength,

---

[1] Marcel Lobot, *Claudel à l'Académie*.
[2] Cingria.

and Mauriac with all his grace. On his feet, with his notes in one hand and holding the microphone in the other like a bishop with his pastoral staff, Claudel spoke for seventy minutes without once touching his glass of water."[1]

The panegyric by his predecessor Louis Gillet gave him the chance to speak of his book on *The Artistic History of the Mendicant Orders,* and by this means give a wide, vivid and symbolic account of the role played by each of the great medieval orders. The *Opus Dei,* which is characteristic of the Order of St. Benedict and, as Claudel told us, "makes the Scriptures vocal," was followed by the "colonizing policy" of the mendicant orders, the brown animal (St. Francis) and the black and white animal (St. Dominic).

The first of these aimed at recalling the world to the Crucified who had come to him in the form of a seraph. It is the cross itself which comes down from the wall to meet the saint, after which to meet the whole of humanity "invited to offer itself with its four limbs" for God to work on it in this way. The other, Dominic, came "to spread fire over the earth," and his black and white habit is the livery of the invincible principle of contradiction.

Mauriac rose and replied, speaking of Gillet and Rimbaud, but doing homage above all to the man who had just been elected. He referred to the dis-

[1] C. d'Ydewalle; *Claudel est entré dans l'immortalité* (*La Nation belge,* March 15, 1947).

tinguished representative of France in the East and
in the West, and to the notable services he had
rendered to the State and to his country. These services were, however, surpassed by those which the poet
had rendered to the spirit of his contemporaries.
Each of us, said Mauriac, owes you something within
his soul. For what benefits? You have brought us
happiness.

No easy happiness, certainly, but a high one, pure
and in accordance with faith. Mauriac finished with
these words, "When you leave this life . . . you
will have the assurance that your work will continue
to remind young men who have lost the light and
are seeking for it, of their royal origin and the love
for which they were created, for a long time after
you have left them behind."

The speaker went far beyond the bounds of a simple
literary eulogy, as he praised Claudel for so nobly
spreading abroad the divine joy, thus being the bene-
factor of generations present and to come. On that
day, as a journalist summed it up, Isaias in person
was received in a green coat.

There were numbers of photographs of the new
academician in the papers and reviews. One of them
attracted my attention. It showed little Marie-Victoire
Nantet admiring her grandfather's smart uniform.
With a timid but charmingly graceful hand, she was
half-opening the broad lapel embroidered with palms,
under the beaming eyes of the poet.

I felt I must do a little water-color of this for such a delightful child. I added these words: Men have crowned the forehead, but she has found the heart.

In her grandfather's friendly letter one can discern his loving heart, and one can imagine him following the "little quail" with his eyes, as she jumped about picking the berries.

CHATEAU DE BRANGUES
Morestel-Brangues
May 28, 1947

My dear Sister,

Little Marie-Vic was proud and delighted with the lovely picture you sent her and she refuses to be separated from it. She spends her time laughing, dancing and beating her wings like a little quail in the paradise which God has given us, the country at this season, and she only has to open her little beak for strawberries and all sorts of good things to fall into it.

Thank you for your charming letter and the moving poem enclosed with it.

My speech at the *Académie* on which you congratulate me tired me very much and left me with an attack of bronchitis which has been curiously difficult to shake off. It looks as if the coming season has yet other tiring experiences in store for my eighty years. I hope that *The Tidings Brought to Mary*, after being massacred so many times without its success being affected, is at last going to receive the kind of production it should have. There will also be my big book on the Song of Songs (nearly 600 pages) to be published. The one on the rosary which I have sent you is very important; there are ideas about the Blessed Virgin which should be studied carefully.

I am going to Rouen tomorrow for the Joan of Arc celebrations, where they are to do *Jeanne au bûcher*. The Cœcilia players from Antwerp are also giving it in Paris on June 13th.

With affection and respect,

P. CLAUDEL

The old man of nearly eighty years was still splendidly active. At that age the journey from Brangues to Rouen was no light matter, and yet, seven years later, he was to go as far as Hamburg! At Brangues, though it was holiday time, he was never idle. There must have been so many things and so much childish laughter to distract him from his work, but, always faithful to his calling, like St. Matthew, he continued to "plough his field of fresh paper."

This "field" was the vast garden of the Song of Songs, the large and solid commentary on which would soon be appearing, a great poem in praise of the Queen of Heaven, as *The Rose and the Rosary* had been.

He would not be meeting her empty-handed.

As I write this, I am thinking of the magnificent letter he wrote to Madame José-Maria Sert, after the death of her husband in December, 1945. It is well known how this great decorative artist on three occasions had the courage to start again on the decoration of the cathedral of Vich in Catalonia, first of all destroyed by fire and then by the hands of revolutionaries. His broad touches of bitumen on a background

of mat gold had a greatness and a lyrical quality all
their own.

Claudel had a great liking and admiration for him.
In the letter of condolence which he sent to his widow
he said, among other things, "I wept all through the
night . . . I had no idea I loved him so much. Do
you remember the day when I came to luncheon
with Sert and he was late? How he suddenly came
into the room with that kind of flickering light on
his face? He was holding a sheet of paper in his hand.
It was the superb drop-scene which he had designed
for *The Satin Slipper*. His hands were still black with
charcoal. For my part, I was looking with emotion
and respect at those hands which had produced so
many masterpieces.

"And I thought at the time: When he appears
before God, when the Blessed Virgin presents him
to her Son, he will only have to show his blackened
hands, the hands of a craftsman, generous hands, and
say, 'This have I done with these hands which you
gave me, along with my eyes, my brain and my heart.' "

These were fine words of praise, both moved and
moving, coming from a brother artist. Could they
not be also applied to their author? When he appeared
before God . . . he had only to show those hands
which had worked so hard, those hands which were
moved by the brain of a genius and a truly great
heart. This is what they have done: they have served
France, they have served the Church, they have served

God and souls, and they will never cease to sow for the generations to come the seed which *is not of death but of light*.[1]

The sowing of light had fallen on the soul which I was preparing for Baptism, the time for which was drawing near. When I told my godfather about it, he wrote me these few lines, which he accompanied with the text of the *Odes* just mentioned.

> 11 Boulevard Lannes (XVI)
> March 31, 1948

My dear Sister,

Many thanks for your kind letter and with all my heart I wish you a happy Easter.

I am sending back to you the two books which I have inscribed and all my congratulations to the fine soul whom you have rescued from that dreadful Luther!

Tidings, for the first time produced as I would wish, is a great success, due especially to a little Belgian actress whom I discovered and who is playing as Mara.

Blessed be our Lord Jesus Christ.[2]

> P. CLAUDEL

A few weeks later, as Claudel was to give a lecture in Brussels on Romain Rolland, he needed some theological statements on the presence of God, and he asked us, in the most simple manner, to check them for him.

---

[1] *Non point de mort, mais de lumière* (*Cinq Grandes Odes*, p. 93).

[2] Claudel's words are: *Et vive Notre-Seigneur Jésus-Christ.*

CHATEAU DE BRANGUES
Morestel-Brangues
June 6, 1948

My dear Sister,

I have been invited by Queen Elizabeth to give a lecture next October on my friend Romain Rolland, which I shall call *L'Itinéraire religieux de Romain Rolland*.[1]

I shall above all be dealing with the question of the agreement between the sense of the immanence of God (according to St. Paul's words, *In Deo vivimus et movemur et sumus*[2]), and that of his transcendence.

On this subject I have come across the following text in a recent and remarkable book on St. Teresa of Avila, who seems to be an authority, "God is present in us by his presence, by his power, and by his essence."

Would the Abbé H, who is a specialist in these high studies, be so kind as to explain this for me? He will then add to all the things for which I am already in his debt.

I do not forget you, my dear Sister, and I often think of the happy hours I spent with you at Bruges.

I hope that your family are keeping well.

With respectful greetings,

P. CLAUDEL

I made a collection of texts from the *Summa* of St. Thomas which I copied out and sent to Claudel with this letter . . .

Very dear godfather,

Your card really touched me with its simplicity. I hastened to copy out for you the most important passages

---

[1] Romain Rolland's religious travel-diary.
[2] It is in him that we live, and move, and have our being.

from the *Summa* which speak of the presence of God. How clear and how deep they are! You will draw marvelous things from them. Furthermore, I have seen the Canon who is back from a journey and he has agreed to my sending you some notes which I took last year when he gave some lectures on the attributes of God. They are really a commentary on St. Thomas, who remains the solid foundation all the time. Dealing with this subject the Canon gave us a commentary on Psalm 128. He is certain to make things clear for you and to open up wide perspectives.

I confess that I felt shy at undertaking this research on your behalf, as if there were anything we could teach you, when you have already attempted and expressed this in all your works, in *Presence and Prophecy* above all.

I imagine that at Brangues your library is not so well supplied as in Paris and that . . . "the Angel of Brangues" has no *Summa* to lend you.

In any case it was a real pleasure to copy out these extracts for you, hoping that they are what you want.

We had the joy, the other day, to hear the records of *Jeanne au bûcher.* The wave of hatred surrounding Joan is well brought out by the music, while she, so fair and so pure, is clothed in flame as if it were a wedding dress. We all greatly enjoyed and appreciated the words and the music.

During the last few days I have been able to act as your apostle to a group of young Swiss admirers. Were you not in Geneva last week? You can see how I follow your movements from a distance, while you are always present in my thought and in my prayers. Tomorrow, the feast of St. Paul, they will be with you even more than usual, asking God to shower his graces and his blessings on you.

Most affectionately in Xto.

This little card thanked me for the papers:

Brangues

Many thanks, my dear Sister, for your letter which will be most useful to me. What a pity that all the books from which you quote are for me like fruits hanging on the tree of Tantalus!

With heartfelt thanks,

P. CLAUDEL

One day was standing out on the horizon, and I did not intend to let it pass, the poet's eightieth birthday. He was certain to receive lovely presents from his family and his friends; there could be no question of my keeping up with them, but when pockets are empty the heart becomes ingenious. With Claudel's long career of travel in mind, I put together a little album with a scarlet cover, in which the story of the poet's *curriculum vitae* was told in pictures, and gave it the subtle title of *Around the World in Eighty Years*. The world stood out on a red background surrounded by several of the planets.

In order to follow this journey round the world, all that was necessary was to open and to unroll the tape, which was more than two yards long. One followed step by step the many picturesque stages covered by the traveler, and beneath each were lines by the poet, referring to the place represented.

The series naturally started with Villeneuve-sur-Fère, with its little rural church tower. Next, there was a young boy perched on a tree, with his eyes scanning the horizon. "I can see myself on the highest branch . . ." Prize-books and laurels recalled Renan's embrace. Then came the silhouette of Notre-Dame de Paris with these words, "It was then that the event occurred which has dominated my whole life . . ." After that, keeping to chronological order, the sky scrapers of New York, "the palaces colored by care"[1] and the Chinese pagodas, the Holy Land, the black line of the Trans-Siberian railway smoking in the snow, the Child Jesus of Prague, Ligugé . . . the film went on unrolling itself. "The mountains have taken vows."[2] We are in Norway. "There is nothing as blue as Florence . . ." After the palm-trees of Rio, the snow-capped summit of Fujiyama, "The Angel of Japan has put on his surplice of feathers."[3] Finally, after America and Brussels, the last port of call was at Brangues, "that syllable of bronze coined three times a day by the Angelus,"[4] without forgetting, in their proper place, the silhouette of *Le Soulier de Satin*, the academic sword, and even the roofs of our convent.

A rather special letter went with the album.

August 2, 1948

To my godfather,

At that time the bells were rung because a child had been born.

[1] *Les palais couleur de souci.*
[2] *Les montagnes ont pris l'habit.*
[3] *L'Ange du Japon a revêtu son surplis de plumes.*
[4] *Cette syllabe de bronze monnayée trois fois le jour par l'Angélus.*

Quid putas puer iste erit? people said to each other.

On that August day the liturgy sang of the splendor of the Son of God transformed on Mount Thabor. He looked down with his dazzling face on the cradle of the new-born child, with two venerable characters, one on each side of him, Moses and Elias.

The Gospel, the Law, the Prophets.

A spiritual and literary vocation began to take shape, while the Father in heaven said of the baptized child, *Hic est filius meus dilectus Paulus.*

Eighteen years later the Lord Jesus met this child who had become a young man. The vocation of the pilgrim was decided then and there, the exile by profession who was to follow the roads from one hemisphere to the other, guided by the *Stella Maris,* telling of the sacred texts to men of all colors.

On this August 6, 1948, a man of eighty years who is looking over his spectacles as the long parchment of his life is unrolled. This humble and light-hearted *Itinerarium* sets out to trace the stages for him over again. May he be able, through these fugitive and imperfect pages, to understand how attached his god-child is to him, full of gratitude and affection. May he see in them the expression of her faithful prayer on his eightieth birthday, and that of the whole community.

Ad multos annos!

With all my heart in Xto.

I must own that I was fairly sure of my little success. In fact, the answer which I received immediately told me so in a charming way: the patriarch was as amused as a child with these riddles. The whole family, always numerous at Brangues on that day, had to look at the album!

In that crowd of children and grandchildren, the kind father made no distinction between those nearest to him and the god-daughter far away, whose good wishes were mingled with theirs, and this will help to understand one delightful little remark. We cannot fail to notice the delicacy with which he was able to open his heart.

CHATEAU DE BRANGUES
Morestel-Brangues
August 5, 1948

Dear Sister A,

The whole family, gathered round the patriarch, gave little cries of joy when they looked at your little album. In my case I could feel, as I turned from one picture to the other, something permanent deep down within me, indefinably gay and innocent—that which makes us children of God and brings one into such complete harmony with Sister A.

It was worth waiting eighty years to find such a friend, and on who is so skillful with her brush dipped in the sun's ray.[1]

What a pity that I have not got the right to embrace you!

P

Soon, perhaps, I may have to ask you for something important.

As can be imagined, such kind encouragement had put me on my mettle, and on the following New

---

[1] From the *Éventails.*

Year's Day I did my best to illustrate my letter of good wishes. This won for me the following reply . . .

> 11 Boulevard Lannes (16e)
> January 12, 1949

My dear God-daughter,

Many thanks for your charming letter and the delightful little drawing which rejoiced my fatherly heart. May God protect you and all your sisters, whom I look upon as my own, in this year of grace 1949.

I have just published two considerable books: a commentary on the Song of Songs and a translation (in my own fashion!) of a choice taken from the psalms.

I cannot remember if I sent them to you. Let me know (a postcard will do).

And once again every good wish from the aching prophet!

> P. CLAUDEL

It took me several months to study and to appreciate fully the biblical and poetic riches of that large *Commentary on the Song of Songs*. Certain imaginary dialogues between the Blessed Virgin and her Son are of outstanding beauty owing to their mystical depth and also their lyrical qualities à le Claudel.

> May 17, 1949

Very dear godfather,

I have just finished reading your translation of the psalms, and how lively and stimulating it is. I so much like your rendering of the long Psalm 118, which could

have been tedious, but from which you have drawn out
such surprising and novel ideas. "I am there, in the light
of the rising sun, steaming like newly ploughed land . . .
The silence listens as it expresses itself little by little, oh
my God, listen to me as I live by you."[1] And those
wicked men who "move sideways like crabs"! David would
be delighted with this metaphor.

What can one say of your commentary on the Song of
Songs? Chapters like the eighth and above all the sixth
plunge into the depths of the union with God with an
insight that is most impressive. The intimacy between
Mary and her Son, such as you describe in verse four,
"Turn your eyes away from me" shows us so well the
need which the Creator and his creature have of each
other, and in the end the unique, transcendent action
of the former in the latter. We do not utter the name
of Jesus without the aid of the Holy Spirit, so St. Paul
tells us. In fact, the smallest act of love which we may
think is most our own is really brought into being by
God. You make this clear in your pages, godfather, and
one feels that it has all been lived and experienced.

I greatly like, on page 265, "this supreme corolla where
the Holy Spirit lays by stores of pollen, of gold and of
purity" . . . and also, on page 273, "this tribe of little
lambs in clouds of tulle which the compassionate eye of
the grandfather beholds from behind his column."[2] We
know him well, this grandfather, I can see him in a

[1] The French, like a certain amount of Claudel's writings, is
obscure. *Je suis là, dans le soleil levant, tout fumant comme une
terre labourée . . . Econte le silence peu à peu qui s'exprime, O
mon Dieu, écoute-moi vivre de Toi.*

[2] Once again, all is a little obscure, so we give the French, p.
265. *Cette corolle suprême où le Saint-Esprit s'approvisionne de
pollen, d'or et de blancheur,* p. 273. *Cette tribu de petits agneaux
en nuages de tulle que l'oeil attendri du grand-père contemple der-
rière son pilier.*

photograph on my table, holding François and Bobinette in his arms . . . near to Marie-Sygne and six other boys and girls who are dear to his heart. How delightful it is.

Dear godfather, please believe in my faithful affection for you in God and in my fervent prayers.

Your god-daughter

Along with my letter I sent some illustrations for the *Eventails* in which I had tried to express that imponderable poetry with its Eastern fragrance. I received the following reply . . .

May 20, 1949

My dear Sister,

Many thanks for your letter.

I like your vignettes immensely, and I dream of having a collection of my poems published, illustrated entirely by you!

With all my heart,

P. CLAUDEL

A TIME TO KEEP SILENCE

To my shame, in spite of my desire to comply with such an invitation, I have never had the courage to embark on this work. The fear of not being up to the work paralyzed me for a long time, and when I was ready to undertake it, our dear poet was leaving us for the other world.

The following year, which was the Holy Year of 1950, Claudel had the special privilege of reading his poems in the Vatican before Pope Pius XII. These two exceptional men had been close friends for a long time. It would have been moving indeed to see the eighty-year-old poet at the feet of the Head of the Church, with an equal mixture of affection and respect, to whom he had devoted several impressive articles.

"It is not enough to know he is there," wrote Claudel, "today we must see him, speak to him, touch him and unite ourselves with him."[1]

In another article, from which I venture to quote a part, the attachment of this true son of the Church

[1] *Gazette de Liège*, April 9, 1950.

for its head is one of the most striking evidences of his faith and his deep understanding of the enormous responsibilities which the Holy Father bears on his shoulders from the day when he is chosen for the tiara.

Recalling the day of his enthronement in March, 1939, Claudel tells us of the emotion he felt, when in the presence of one on whom he looked not as a sovereign but as a victim . . . a prisoner of love, a prisoner of his papal crown, holding out his arms to the cheering crowd.

"For eleven years," wrote Claudel in 1950, "never once were those sacred arms, those saving arms, lowered . . . and when great weariness would have made them sag, the cross was there, unbending, unrelenting, to keep them opened out and lifted up."

(What was this cross, if not "this horrible war, stretching to the ends of the earth"?)

"But," the poet added, "the tyrants have gone. Rome, at one moment threatened, has been miraculously spared. Are we at last going to give some respite to those outstretched arms? Less than ever. In the East yet another Cain has appeared, more hideous, more dangerous than his predecessors . . . whole Christian peoples have been delivered over to him, whom he holds under his abominable sway. . . . Do not lower your arms, son of Man, for we know that we cannot seek our salvation in the atomic bomb or in the decomposition of hydrogen, but from the answer which will be made to the intimate question God is himself asking the man who has succeeded him on the cross: *Peter, dost thou love me?* You see all these men who hate me, all these blind men who insult me, all these weak men who think they are honoring me when they mumble a name which means nothing to them. And you, my son, do you love me more than these others?"

Such a noble page needs no commentary. For us also it is rather an "intimate question" which our whole lives as convinced Christians should answer.

The following June, I sent my usual good wishes for his feastday, and I alluded to this fine piece of writing.

My letter had, of course, to be illustrated with little vignettes . . . The winding course of the Tiber . . . The basilica of St. Paul without the walls . . . The dove in the pontifical coat of arms.

After that our correspondence spaced out over a period of silence and recollection. Discretion made me observe a certain restraint towards this aged man, and I also had plenty of work and a good many letters to write. When I ventured to send a short letter now and then, Claudel would reply with some work which had just appeared, and a fatherly dedication would reassure me that I was not forgotten. It is necessary that in human friendships there should be these periods of rest, giving an element of distance to the relationship, in the course of which they grow deeper. These periods are the touchstone of true affection, which does not grow less but becomes all the stronger.

Tempus loquendi, say the Scriptures, *et tempus tacendi*.

At the beginning of 1951, Claudel sent me a copy of his *Gospel of Isaias*,[1] and I thanked him.

April 26, 1951

My dear godfather,

It is a great joy, from the first page of your *Isaias*, to be taken hold of by that astonishingly young and vigorous hand, your hand, dear godfather, combined with that of the prophet, and to know that it will not let go! Indeed, you do not let me go, and you continue to spoil your god-child by sending her so faithfully the echo of the best in your thought.

I had been hoping for a long time that you would devote a work to Isaias, that splendid giant, the fore-runner of the writers of the Gospels, the "strange en-thusiast who had compassion on God."[2] Our age still stands in his need. The bourgeois goes on growling out *non petam*, whereas, on the three Rogation Days, our Lord repeats to us, *petite* and we sing *Te rogamus audi nos . . .* Dear godfather, if only could you come to one of our morning processions, in the freshness of a spring day, with narcissi and jonquils all around and lawns sparkling with dew, while the praise of the rising sun is mingled with our prayers, a splash of light in the tur-quoise-blue of the dawn . . . to say nothing of the pigeons as they coo and display their fan-tails round their dove-cote.

---

[1] *Evangile d'Isaïe.*
[2] The French is again highly obscure. *Cette espèce d'enragé qui a eu pitié de Dieu.*

Thank you with all my heart for your present. You know how I will value and read and meditate about it. This silly little sketch will prove this to you[1] . . . but there are some others which are more sensible!

I thought of you when poor Gide died, and I prayed for him. What judgment will he receive from God?

Your grateful god-daughter.

In 1953 he sent me a copy of *A Voice Out of Israel*,[2] an echo of the atrocities committed during the war, and with it this letter.

11 Boulevard Lannes (XVI)
January 28, 1953

My dear Sister,

Many thanks for your letter with the charming pictures! Indeed I have not forgotten you and I am conscious of your prayers which accompany me all the time.

Please give my religious and affectionate greetings to your sisters.

All is well here.

I am sending you my latest book, written during the most dreadful moments of the last war.

With all my heart in Xto Jesu,

P. CLAUDEL

In the course of that 1953 both our families were saddened by bereavement, for I lost my father and

---

[1] A rather outlandish husband and wife illustrated the passage in *L'Evangile d'Isaïe*: "The formidable depths of matter in which the atom weds the electron," with these words, "Will you be my isotope?"

[2] *Une voix sur Israïl.*

Claudel his son-in-law, Jacques Paris, who was killed in a car accident. You might think, on reading his reply to my letter of condolence, that Claudel scarcely felt this. This seeming coldness was however deliberate, the sign of deep feelings which he did not wish to show.

11 Boulevard Lannes (XVI)
January 22, 1954

My dear Sister,

Thank you for your good wishes and your prayers. You are often in my thoughts. I understand so well how you feel about your father. I thought he had completely returned to religion. Not so? Mine died without the Sacraments, and as far as outward appearances went, was always "far away." But I have never ceased to trust in the Father.

He is above all things a *father*: more loving even than the best of our good priests whom we know. And his Son died for us. Of what use would this be, if it was only for "good" Christians?

I also have lost my son-in-law, Jacques Paris, who was Secretary-General of the Council of Europe. He was killed at the same time as his mother in a car accident, when they were going on a pilgrimage to Le Verdelain. He leaves a widow and five children. Pray for them all and for your old friend,

P. Claudel

I think it must have been about this time that he had the first warnings of the heart complaint which would kill him the following year.

He never breathed a word of this in his letters, so that we had come to think that he might be invulner-

able. But the hour, which he had been thinking about
for a long time, was about to sound. He had prepared
to the full for this last journey, from which no traveler
returns. It would be difficult to garner from all his
works the little rehearsals for this last act. Consider
these lines from *Le 25 décembre 1886*, where the poet
examines his conscience before the Virgin, this tenta-
tive discovery of the world which he made constantly
from one end of the world to the other . . .[1]

> All this paper
> which has accumulated behind me
> Some calls for tears
> some for laughter!
> What a terrible experience—
> to be forced to read it all over again
>
> If only we could reach an agreement,
>   my Dear,
> which would guarantee that you would regard
> all I have done
> all I have written
> as nothing at all
> And that when I appear before you
> I'll be fortunate enough to stand there
> without a mark on me
> encumbered no longer
> Free finally of this insipid literature!

[1] The French is again obscure . . . *cette découverte du monde
à tâtons qu'il a essayé de faire d'un bout du monde à l'autre.*

But allow me this much
to wait in quiet thought
for what is certain to happen before long
Like somebody about to undergo a
catastrophe
(for example, raise his eyes and see you)
Who must be playing out a fearful part
because he acts like he is made without fear[1]

This poem is dated 1942, not 1955. This Christian soul would not be alarmed when the Master "knocked at the door . . ."

The moment was no longer far away. We were in January 1955. I had recently read *Les mémoires improvisés*, and I was thinking of sending Claudel a summary of my impressions. I can remember that I had taken up a rather frivolous attitude, comparing this dialogue with Jean Amarouche to the fable of the lion and the gnat, as he tormented his partner with questions.

January 14, 1955

My dear godfather,

I wanted to write to you earlier to send you my good wishes for the New Year, but I waited till I had finished reading your *mémoires improvisés* so as to give you my impressions, for what they are worth. I have hopes they may perhaps amuse you, though they were written down

[1] *Visages radieux*, pp. 24–27. The French has an untranslatable play on the words *et qui fait semblant, semblant fait de ne pas avoir peux.*

hurriedly, for I have not had much leisure to revise them carefully. I send them to you in the complete intimacy of a god-daughter to her godfather . . .

When I am in the mood to complain, I think of the unique good fortune I had to find in your faithful and affectionate friendship and in the great things of your thought, the most effective levers in my religious life.

Dear godfather, you must forgive me if I am carried away by a little poetic enthusiasm. But, I think I may dare say anything to a man of eighty-six years who has wielded over me something like the power of a father? It is certain that if I had not met you, my life would have been completely different . . . and, who knows, perhaps unhappy? God alone knows, and may he be blessed for it.

I know that for several years you have been so kind as to send me one of your books as a New Year's present or for my birthday. You know how much happiness this gives me. If I may tell you what I would like best, I would so much like to have *Cent phrases pour èventails*, which is the most perfect thing you have written. In case you have no more copies of this, I would be so glad to have *Seigneur apprenez-nous à prier* or *Conversations dans le Loir-et-Cher*.

If you have neither the one nor the other, then I leave it to you. Everything which comes from you is a pleasure. Meanwhile, very many thanks, all my good wishes for a happy and holy year, with the promise of my faithful prayers.

Your god-daughter

A *holy year* . . . it was to be that of his death. A few lines traced out with a shaking hand brought me his last thoughts, and offered me his last presents.

11 Boulevard Lannes (XVI)
January 26, 1955

My dear Sister,

Thank you for your kind letter and the pages you sent with it. I am ill and cannot write anything longer.

I am having the three books in question sent to you. Soon my other ones. Pray for me.

P. CLAUDEL

"Pray for me," this was his last request to his god-daughter, at the threshold of death. She has tried to be faithful to it.

A few days later, I had a letter from a dress-designer at the *Comédie Française* telling me that *L'Annonce faite à Marie* was to be performed in that theater on February 17, and asking me for exact particulars of our medieval dress which was to be worn by Violaine. This I sent to her.[1]

There followed the incredible success of the play, which was highly praised by President Coty and also by the Press. The poet had a real *apotheosis*, and there were long notices in the papers.

Six days later, on February 23, at the beginning of Lent, the radio announced in the morning that on the night before the poet had given back his soul to God. There was world-wide emotion. The aged patriarch had left for another glory, one finer yet and to which there is no end.

[1] The community to which the author belongs are active modern Benedictine nuns, but they wear the habit of the medieval Beguines.

"Let me die quietly. I am not afraid."

These were his last words, a striking reminder of the poem quoted above. I wrote a long remembrance to a friend, in reply to her letter of condolence. Here are parts of it:

His life was for me a perpetual absence, whereas his death is a presence.

In all his works there is a cry of desire for Heaven. He was haunted by this, and his life was devoted to it.

He made me grow accustomed to finding him only beyond that light veil where souls are transparent to each other.

Furthermore, I had no need to look elsewhere. He was there where I was in the habit of looking for him.

If the funeral trappings gave the appearance of mourning, three sublime women had come together to clothe them with splendor: Our Lady, the Church, and France. They offered him shelter in the most sacred, most honorable and most impressive place, the choir of Notre-Dame, the heart of Mary.

In the very same place where her smile had once conquered a young and impetuous adolescent, she was again welcoming him, a gentle mother about to rock his last slumber and to invite him to the "Feast of Wisdom," the reward of fidelity.

"It is joy which is the strongest," sang Joan in the midst of the flames, in her apotheosis as a national

heroine. And that same song our catholic poet is singing to us from beyond the grave.

His god-daughter

Later, in the glory of autumn, his body was
solemnly buried. "Fresh and green are the pastures
where he gives me rest," sang the psalmist.

On September 2, the coffin left the sanctuary of
Notre-Dame, and was taken across France to the
banks of the Rhone. He had asked to be buried there.

An interestingly mixed assembly was present: a
Cardinal, some academicians, well-known artists, peas-
ants from the neighborhood, all joined his family,
unified by the same feeling of affection for the great
man whom they were laying to rest.

Many people had undertaken to keep vigil during
the night in the church, which proved too small to
house all those who came there for the funeral.

Then, when the absolutions were over, the proces-
sion went out across the countryside, in the clear
autumn sunshine, to the grave which was on his
property.

"The wonderful world which surrounded us," wrote
Daniel-Rops who was there that day, "with nature
so beautiful and so pure in its lines, so delicate in its
colors, had no need of words or dogmas for one to
be convinced in the depths of one's being that it was
indeed the visible image of another, ineffable splendor,

to which, by means of sign and symbol, the whole
of Claudel's work has borne witness."[1]

In that place his body will now rest, lulled by the
distant song of the great river.

> He comes forth
> not from the earth
> He comes down from the sky[2]

I see him there surrounded by rough grass and wild
flowers, watched over by the trembling poplar, like
a candle that never sleeps, waiting in place for the
happy resurrection of his ashes—the seed of eternity
and glory.

> *Face to face in the love which is my*
>   *end,*
> *in the Cause which is*
>   *Truth*
> *There only shall I find my*
>   *home.*

"In my flesh I shall see God," said Job, "I shall
see him myself and not another. And my eyes will
gaze upon him. There lies my hope. It dwells in my
bosom."

> Here rest
> *The remains and the seed*
> *of Paul Claudel*[3]

---

[1] Nocturnes, published in 1956 by Grasset.

[2] *La Messe là-bas.*

[3] His epitaph . . . *Ici reposent les restes et la semence de Paul Claudel.*

A NOTE ON THE TYPE

IN WHICH THIS BOOK WAS SET

This book has been set in Electra, a type face created in 1935 by W. A. Dwiggins, the well-known Boston artist. This type falls within the "modern" family of type styles, but was drawn to avoid the extreme contrast between "thick and thin" elements that marks most "modern" type faces. The design is not based upon any traditional model, and is not an attempt to revive or to reconstruct any historic type. Since its birth, Electra has met with success because of its easy-to-read quality. This book was composed and printed by the York Composition Company, Inc., of York, Pennsylvania and bound by Moore and Company of Baltimore. The design and typography of this book are by Howard N. King.